STEP-BY-STEP # weaving

A COMPLETE INTRODUCTION TO THE CRAFT OF WEAVING

INCLUDING PHOTOGRAPHS IN FULL COLOR

by Nell Znamierowski

DESIGNED BY AND PRODUCED UNDER

THE SUPERVISION OF WILLIAM AND SHIRLEY SAYLES

GOLDEN PRESS · NEW YORK

FOREWORD

Here is a book that teaches weaving in an interesting, simple, and direct manner. As a weaver myself, closely associated with textile design and with weavers in industry, I consider the beginner fortunate to be introduced to the world of hand-weaving by means of this instructive book.

Handweaving is fascinating to most people but attempted by relatively few, probably because it seems more complex than it is. As in all crafts, a basic interest is required before the first step toward instruction is taken. Once the decision has been made to pursue this rewarding craft, it is most important to obtain a proper background of fundamental knowledge. In this book, Nell Znamierowski has successfully projected all essentials of handweaving, including an imaginative and contagious flair for pattern, texture, color, and good taste.

A unique feature of this book is the presentation of step-by-step projects, including adaptations of designs which were stimulated by Nell Znamierowski's travels in Greece and Finland. Of particular interest is the valuable information she has provided on how to dye yarns.

There are many more dividends in this book that you will discover for yourself.

This is good reading and good weaving.

BOB CARR, VICE PRESIDENT

Jack Lenor Larsen, Inc.

contents

acknowledgments

Among those who have assisted in the preparation of this book, special thanks are due to:

Hal Halverstadt, *Consultant*
Betty MacDonald, *Design*
Louis Mervar, *Photography*
John Giannoni, *Artist*
Olivia Buehl, *Picture Research*

Poncho shirt, 28¼" x 25½", from Middle Paracas Culture (**c.** 600 B.C.) of Peru, woven in tapestry technique of alpaca wool. (Collection of the Textile Museum, Washington, D.C. ; photo courtesy Museum of Primitive Art, New York)

INTRODUCTION

Weaving can be defined simply as the interlacing of threads at right angles to form a web or fabric. However, it is much more than this in terms of the excitement and satisfaction that you will find in the actual process of creating a fabric.

This book is written for the new weaver who has access to a floor or table loom and for the potential weaver who has not yet decided whether to invest in a loom. The construction of a simple frame loom, as described in this book, offers the latter a means with which to be initiated into this fascinating craft.

The workings of a handloom and the mechanics of handweaving are easily mastered with a little guidance, encouragement, and application. This book, I hope, will give you the guidance and encouragement. The application will come as you find yourself becoming more and more devoted to this craft.

THE HISTORY OF WEAVING

When we become weavers, our efforts form part of the modern link in the long chain of weaving history that dates back 20,000 years or more. It is thought that early man first used the weaving process by criss-crossing and intertwining twigs, reeds, and rushes. Later, as he became acquainted with other fibers and animal hairs, he employed these also in his rough works.

Throughout the centuries of evolution that followed, the spindle and the loom were developed—the former in the attempts to obtain a longer continuous thread from the fibers and animal hairs, and the latter as a stable fixture on which to attach these threads. Types of looms varied from area to area rather than from century to century. The ancient Greeks seemed to prefer the same type of upright loom, on which one weaves from the top down, as did some North American Indian tribes and the early Scandinavians. Egyptian weavers of about 2500 B.C. used another type of upright, or vertical, loom similar to that of the later Persians, and also a horizontal loom, such as was used by the Incas and is still used today in Mexico, Guatemala, and Peru. Whatever loom was employed, the principle remained the same—passing and interlocking a weft, or horizontal, thread through a stationary warp, or vertical, threads.

Although fabrics of the utmost beauty and sheerness were woven even in the days of the ancients, weaving tools and supplies were in a constant process of refinement in order to further enhance the finished product. Europe, until the time of the early Renaissance, depended on traders and Crusaders to bring her the elaborate textiles from the Far and Near East. Then the Italian weavers mas-

Woman of old Peru weaving on a horizontal backstrap loom, from sixteenth century drawing. (Courtesy the Smithsonian Institution) Man weaving (below) on an upright 2-harness counterbalanced loom, from Mendel's Twelve Brothers Manuscript, 1527. (Courtesy The Bettmann Archive)

tered the intricate weaves and skills of the Orient, as did eventually the French, Spanish, and English, so that they could make their own velvets, damasks, and brocades.

In 18th-century England the drive for increased textile production and ease of operation was continually going on and led eventually to the discoveries that brought about the Industrial Revolution. However, when the first settlers came to America, they had no need of such elegant fabrics and concentrated their labors on plain goods for the simple household and clothing demands of the times.

Research and invention are still an important part of the weaving industry. Some of the new equipment and processes are vastly intricate and complicated, but, as you become more familiar with handweaving, you will see that the basic techniques remain the same whether done on a handloom or a high-speed power loom.

WHY WEAVE?

Although I regard all weaving as allied to the arts, and there are those of you who will want to use it only as a means of self-expression to create beautiful tapestries and wall hangings, weaving also has a very practical side. A purse can be as much an object of beauty as a wall hanging, and the wall hanging as useful as the purse, since it adorns a space that otherwise might be barren. Neither is more lovely than the other and neither is more important to weave.

Smaller items, such as handbags, pillow covers, stoles, and table mats are all useful accessories and make wonderful gifts. There is nothing more pleasant for the giver or receiver than a present made for someone especially in mind. The practical aspect of weaving sometimes can be put to profit, for every year there are more craft shops and fairs springing up around the country. These outlets specialize in selling handwoven items, so perhaps this is your chance to earn some "pin" money.

For those battling an illness, weaving can be a help on the road to rehabilitation. It is a craft long known for its therapeutic value and is becoming increasingly popular in many hospitals.

It is a craft for young and old. As long as the loom is simple and the yarn fairly strong, children are fascinated by weaving and take great pride in the end result. I still remember making potholders on my first simple frame loom, when I was eight or nine years old.

As with all crafts, a certain amount of patience is required, but patience will grow and relaxation settle in as you build up your skills and become intrigued with the interplay of color, the texture of yarns, and the beauty and logic of fabric construction. Unless you are weaving under a deadline, whether you are slow or fast

A simple early Peruvian loom showing a portion of a tapestry band. (Courtesy The American Museum of Natural History)

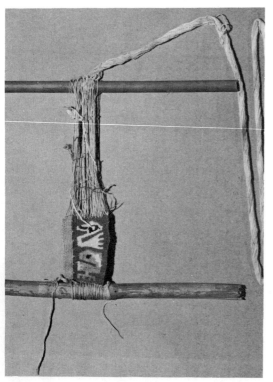

"Cottleston Pie" tapestry, 23" x 26", woven of wool, silk, rayon, and cotton, by Pamela Stearns (Research files of the American Craftsmen's Council).

does not matter. What does matter is the amount of enjoyment and fascination you find in the delight of "doing." This "doing" is a constantly revitalizing process, for, as you watch the woven article develop on your loom, new ideas and endless possibilities for further exploration open up before you.

THE WEAVING PROCESS AND THE HANDLOOM

A fabric, whether it is a rug, tapestry, or suiting material, is made up of a warp and a filling. The warp consists of the lengthwise threads, also called ends. When fabric is held up in front of us, these are the vertical threads. It is this warp that will be interlaced with the filling threads, also called weft. In order to accomplish this interlacing without difficulty and to give pleasing results, the warp is put on a loom in a manner that gives the warp ends even tension.

We all know what darning looks like and how it is achieved by going over and under threads with a needle. Plain weaving is like darning—but without the needle. In place of the needle, a shuttle is used. In weaving, the "over" ends are lifted first while the "under" ends remain stationary. The filling goes through the opening between them. This opening is called the shed. It allows the shuttle, which carries the filling thread, to glide smoothly between the warp ends. These ends are lifted by various means according to the type of loom you have. By repeating this process of lifting a set of ends, passing the filling through, and beating it down into position, you are weaving.

Looms may be of many types, but the basic techniques of weaving remain the same. Shown below is a small table model 2-harness loom.

The loom is the essential commodity in weaving, for there must be a place to stretch the warp. You will need a few other tools, also, some of which can be improvised.

In order to have the warp properly on the loom, there are a few necessary preparatory steps. These include making the warp to the desired width and length on a warping reel or warping board. After the warp is completed it is made into a long chain and transferred to the loom. Here it is rolled onto the warp beam of the loom and then threaded through the heddles and reed. The heddles look like long needles, with the eye of the heddle found in the center. They are attached to the harnesses, the raising or lowering of which gives us the shed. The reed is in the front of the loom. It spaces the warp and beats down the filling.

To complete our preparation, the warp is tied to a front bar of the loom and bobbins are wound and placed in the shuttles. We can then begin weaving.

PLANNING YOUR WOVEN PROJECT

As you become involved with weaving, you will want to plan your own fabrics and woven articles. To aid you in this there are chapters on yarns and color. A working knowledge of the various types of yarns and fibers will guide you in selecting the proper threads in the correct amounts for your planned project.

Color selection and coordination are some of the most pleasurable aspects of weaving and give wide opportunity for your personality to really shine through. However, for those of you who feel a little hesitant or in need of guidance, I have included my own particular methods on how to use color to its fullest advantage. Very often dealing with color brings you to the point of wanting to dye your own shades. This in itself can be a very good exercise in getting to know color and its properties intimately.

Along with choosing your own yarns and colors, you will want to pick out or develop the weave that suits your fabric best. Selecting the weave, the correct threading, and the order in which the harnesses will be raised for the shed openings are all part of the creativeness of weaving. They can best be understood and accomplished by learning how to draft weaves on graph paper. I have given the method I usually use, but in time you will develop your own. Drafting will also help you to understand fabrics already woven.

A LOOM TO MAKE

A very simple loom can be made at home out of a picture frame or a wooden stretcher such as artists use to stretch canvas. It is

Purse woven in plain weave with a finger-manipulated lace technique (See Lace Weaves, pages 74–79).

light, sturdy, and portable and can be used to make rugs, tapestries, purses, and other useful items.

Working on the frame loom will develop a feeling for the weaving process and, in the meantime, thought can be given to exactly the type of work you want to do and what kind of loom you should ultimately buy.

The frame loom can also serve as a second loom for those who have access to a larger one. Once you begin weaving, you will have so many ideas that you want to try out that a single loom may not be enough. It is quite common for weavers to work on more than one project at the same time. But keep in mind that the frame loom is used for 2-harness or finger-manipulated weaves only.

There is a special method of preparing the warp and of weaving on the frame loom, but the principle of interlacing a warp and filling to form a fabric remains the same.

WHAT TO WEAVE

There are so many things to weave and so many different techniques to try that it is often difficult for a beginner to choose the right one as his first work. I have included projects that I feel will give the new weaver a good introduction to the workings of the loom and the possibilities of the woven craft. The first five projects are designed to be woven on either a frame loom or a table or floor loom. The remaining projects are exclusively for a 4-harness table or floor loom, since I hope that eventually you will want to know and experience the pleasure of working on a loom that will allow you to do more complex structures.

None of the projects have to be followed exactly, for, as you begin to feel at home at the loom, you will start to have your own ideas of what you want to explore. I find it a great asset to keep a small notebook handy. In it I jot down color schemes or inspirations for patterns and attach interesting pieces of yarn that I want to try out.

I am a firm believer in sample warps in which you can experiment to your heart's content—and then use the fruits of your experience in your finished piece.

At the conclusion of the book there is a glossary for quick reference and a list of suppliers for looms, other equipment, and yarns. Your experiences in weaving will be, I trust, happy ones so that you will want to go on and broaden your knowledge. There is a list of books, magazines, and museums included for this purpose. Also included is a roster of schools that specialize in summer weaving workshops. There are many others than those I have listed and I am sure that, should you decide to attend one, you will be impressed to see how very active the weaving tradition continues to be.

The frame loom (above) was used to make a section of a rya rug (below). Instructions to make this simple loom are on pages 16–17. For the rya rug directions, see pages 60–65.

LOOMS

A loom is a device that holds the warp ends, or threads, taut so that a shed, or opening, can be formed. Through this shed the filling, or weft, is passed and the interlacing process between warp and filling achieved.

There are simple looms and complex looms. There are rough looms made of tree branches or scrap wood and sleek looms made of the best timber available. But they all must have a shed in order to weave. The way the shed is formed divides all looms into three basic categories.

LOOM BUYING

All the looms mentioned are equally serviceable and the kind you decide to buy depends purely on a matter of personal preference and on what you want to weave. If you want to concentrate on tapestries, harness looms are superfluous. If you are interested in rugs and simple fabrics, nothing over 4 harnesses is needed. For scarves, table mats, and purses, a 27″ loom is more than ample. The cost of the loom is determined by the materials used in making it, the workmanship involved, the width of the loom, and the number of harnesses. Supply sources are listed at the end of this book.

FRAME, UPRIGHT OR VERTICAL, STICK OR BACKSTRAP LOOMS

These are variations of the same type of loom that has no harnesses but has two different shed openings and at least one shed has to be opened by using a shed stick. In some cases, the fingers are used to open the space between two sets of warp ends. Since the fingers are used in our frame loom, this method will be discussed later.

These looms were at one time the only kind of looms, and all others developed from them. In the vertical loom, the warp faces the weaver in an up and down position. Tapestry looms are usually of this type. Backstrap and stick looms, which are primitive looms still used in many parts of Central,

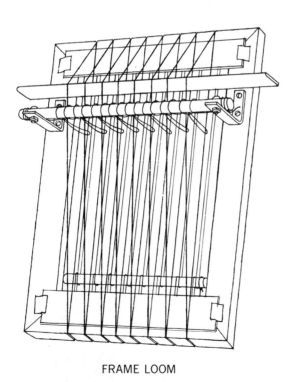

FRAME LOOM

In the Frame Loom, the shed stick is turned on edge to form the first shed.

TAPESTRY LOOM

Upright loom, for making rugs and tapestries. The prongs on top of the loom are used to maintain tension.

South, and North America, are horizontal looms, with the warp running back to front. Frame looms can be either vertical or horizontal, depending on whether they are attached to legs or supports or held in the weaver's lap.

These looms are the slowest to manipulate, but this does not mean that the results are less handsome. The ancient Incas wove on such looms and their fabrics have yet to be surpassed in beauty or technical skill.

TABLE LOOMS

Table looms can have a number of shed openings. The number depends upon the number of harnesses, with the usual range from 2 to 16. The hand is the force that changes and opens the sheds. It does so by pressing on levers, turning knobs, or rotating wheels which in turn raise the harnesses that have the warp strung on them through heddles.

Most table looms come in weaving widths from 8″ to 32″ and are easily transported and stored.

TABLE LOOM
4-harness rising shed table loom. The sheds are opened by pressing on the levers at side of loom.

FLOOR LOOMS

The sheds are made by pressing on foot-controlled treadles, which leaves the hands free to throw and catch the shuttle. These looms are the fastest and most rhythmic of all to operate. They sometimes come with as many as 24 harnesses or as few as 2; 16 is the normal maximum. In this book, we will not be concerned with looms of more than 4 harnesses. The treadles are attached in the under part of the loom to slats of wood called lams. These lams then attach to the harnesses. Pressing on the treadle pulls down on the lam which then either raises or lowers the harness. If it is raised, this is called a rising shed. If it is lowered, the term is sinking shed. Jack type looms are common examples of the former, and counterbalanced looms of the latter. These looms come in weaving widths from 20″ to 60″.

You may possibly come across a countermarch loom, which is a rarity these days. In this loom, the shed operates on both systems at the same time; that is, one set of threads rises as the other sinks.

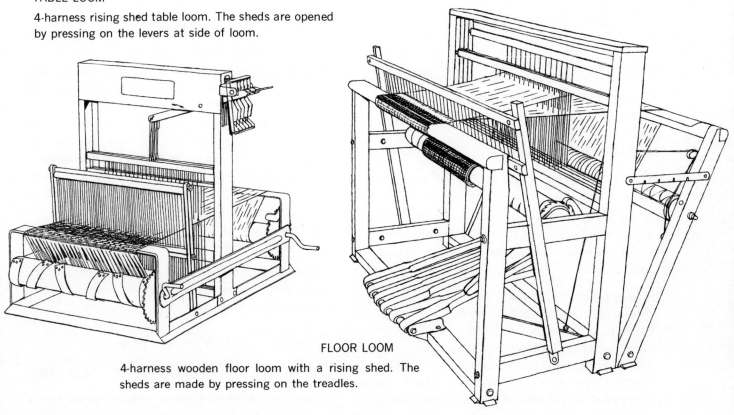

FLOOR LOOM
4-harness wooden floor loom with a rising shed. The sheds are made by pressing on the treadles.

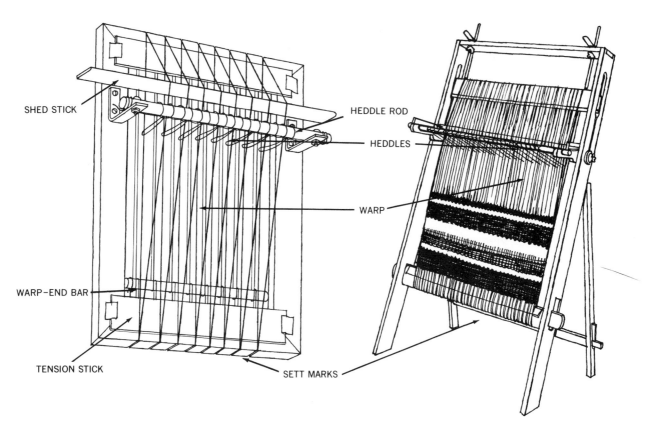

FRAME LOOM   TAPESTRY LOOM

PARTS OF THE LOOM

In order to understand weaving, it is important to know the different parts of the loom. Here, illustrated and explained, are the parts of the frame and upright models.

Frame and Upright Models

In the frame loom the top of the frame serves as the back beam and the bottom as the breast beam. There are no harnesses, treadles, levers, beater, or reed.

Heddles Long loops of string through which the warp passes. They are attached to the heddle rod.
Heddle Rod Carries the heddle loops and can be stationary or movable. Here, it is stationary.
Sett Marks Grooves filed or sawed into the top and bottom frames at ½″ intervals. They take the place of the reed in the table and floor looms. The warp

is spaced between them.
Shed Stick A shed opening is made by turning this stick at a right angle to the warp. It is not attached to the loom.
Warp-end Bar The warp ends revolve around this dowel rod to which are tied the beginning and end of the warp. It is placed at the back of the loom.
Tension Stick Keeps the warp under proper tension for weaving. It is removed as the warp tightens in the process of weaving.
Tapestry Comb Used to beat in the filling. An ordinary comb or fork may be used.

Here, illustrated and explained, are the parts of the table and floor models which, with few exceptions, are the same for both types.

Table and Floor Models

The list reads from the back of the loom to the front.

Warp Beam The rotating lower back beam over which

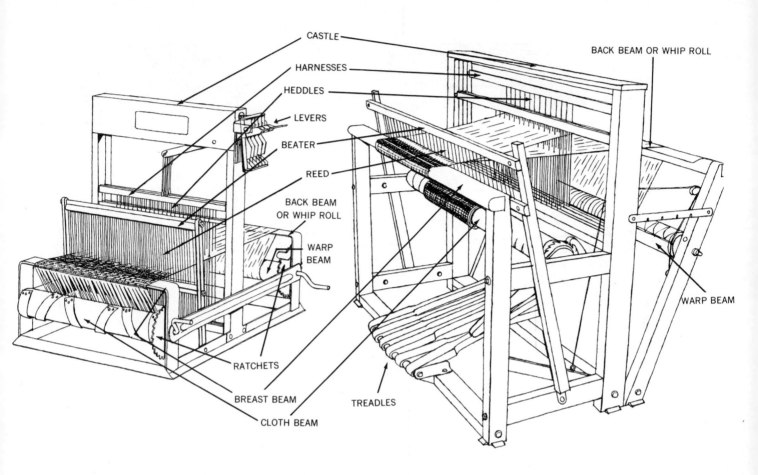

CASTLE

HARNESSES

HEDDLES

LEVERS

BEATER

REED

BACK BEAM
OR WHIP ROLL

WARP
BEAM

BACK BEAM OR WHIP ROLL

WARP BEAM

RATCHETS

BREAST BEAM

CLOTH BEAM

TREADLES

TABLE LOOM   FLOOR LOOM

the unwoven warp is wound and stored.

Apron Bars (not shown) The warp is tied to, or slipped over, the back apron bar. The beginning of the warp is tied to an identical bar at the front.

Apron (not shown) Attaches the apron bar to either warp beam in back or cloth beam in front.

Ratchets Wheels with teeth to maintain the proper tension. One is at the back of the loom and one at the front.

Back Beam or Whip Roll Provides a surface for the warp to glide over and helps to keep the warp at an even tension.

Castle The central main structure of the loom that houses the harnesses.

Harnesses Two horizontal bars between which the heddles are strung.

Heddles Lengths of metal, wire or string that are suspended between the harnesses. They have a center loop, or eye, through which the warp yarn passes.

Levers Located in the upper part of the castle on table looms and attached to the harnesses. Working

them lifts the desired harnesses. In some looms, knobs or wheels perform the same function.

Beater With the reed inserted in it, it beats the filling down.

Reed Comblike device inserted in the beater. It spaces the warp, in slots called dents, according to the width and density that is called for in the finished fabric. Reeds come in various sizes. The size indicates the number of dents per inch and is engraved in the first metal bar on the short side of the reed.

Breast Beam Provides a foundation for the woven web as it moves down to the cloth beam.

Cloth Beam Rolls up the finished cloth as it is woven off.

Treadles Foot pedals that operate harnesses when pressed.

Lams (not shown) Levers lying between the treadles and harnesses and attached to both. Pressing on a treadle pulls on the lams. This in turn raises or lowers the harness to which each lam is attached.

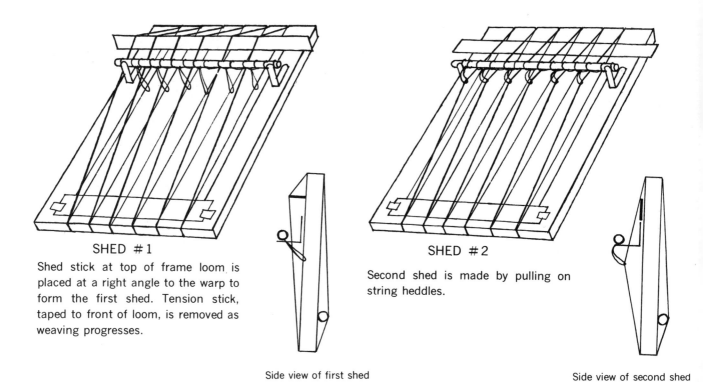

SHED #1

Shed stick at top of frame loom is placed at a right angle to the warp to form the first shed. Tension stick, taped to front of loom, is removed as weaving progresses.

Side view of first shed

SHED #2

Second shed is made by pulling on string heddles.

Side view of second shed

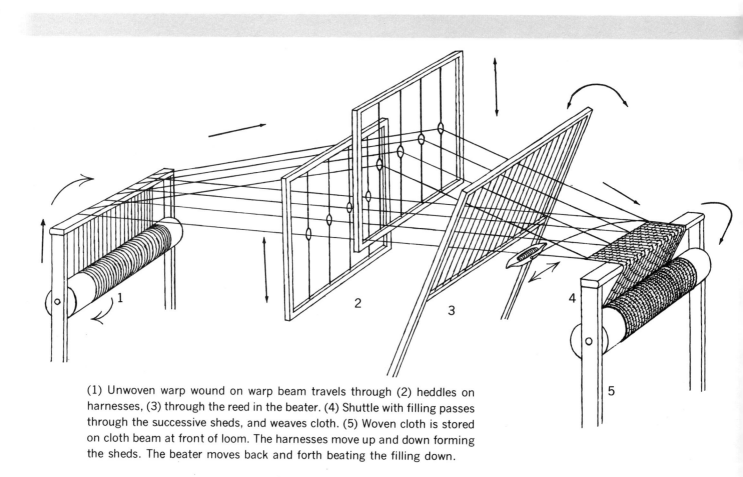

(1) Unwoven warp wound on warp beam travels through (2) heddles on harnesses, (3) through the reed in the beater. (4) Shuttle with filling passes through the successive sheds, and weaves cloth. (5) Woven cloth is stored on cloth beam at front of loom. The harnesses move up and down forming the sheds. The beater moves back and forth beating the filling down.

The Frame Loom

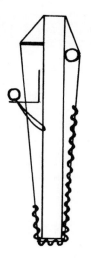

In order to open a shed on the frame loom, the shed stick is turned on edge at a right angle to the warp. From the side, the shed is seen to have a V-shaped passage. The shuttle carries the filling thread through this passage. The shed is closed by returning the shed stick to its original position, and the filling is beaten down with a comb or fork.

The next shed is made by pulling out and up on the string heddles. The filling is reinserted, the shed released, and the filling beaten down again.

As more and more cloth is woven, the shed openings become smaller and additional warp must be made available. One of the front tension sticks is then removed, and the warp-end bar pushed up so that the woven warp revolves around the bottom and up the back of the loom. Weaving is then continued.

Side view of woven cloth
revolving to back of loom

The Table or Floor Loom

The shed is formed by pressing on the treadles, or levers. On a floor loom the treadles are attached to the harness via the lams in the order corresponding to the related sheds. The shuttle glides through the shed with the weaver leaving the thread at a diagonal.

The top of the beater is grasped firmly in the center and pulled forward to beat down the filling. The beater is returned to its original position, the next shed is formed, and the filling beaten down once more. The shuttle is then passed through again.

When more warp is needed in front of the beater, the back ratchet is released. The woven warp is then revolved around the cloth beam until unwoven warp is brought into the weaving position. The back ratchet is resecured so that tension is held once more.

Weaving continues in this rhythmic manner—the harnesses moving up and down and the beater backwards and forwards.

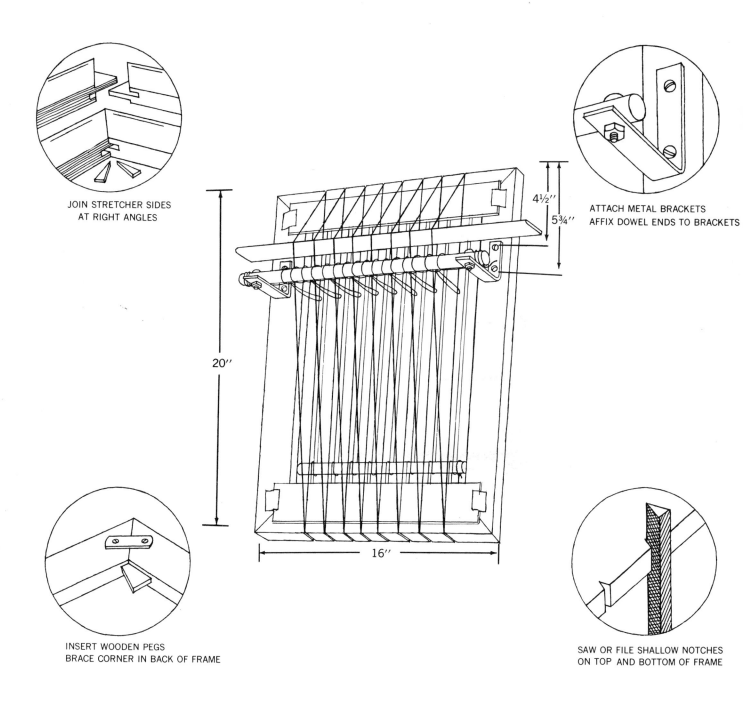

JOIN STRETCHER SIDES
AT RIGHT ANGLES

ATTACH METAL BRACKETS
AFFIX DOWEL ENDS TO BRACKETS

INSERT WOODEN PEGS
BRACE CORNER IN BACK OF FRAME

SAW OR FILE SHALLOW NOTCHES
ON TOP AND BOTTOM OF FRAME

20″

16″

4½″

5¾″

CONSTRUCTION OF THE FRAME LOOM

The frame loom used in this book for the first five projects was made of a wooden stretcher such as artists use to stretch canvas. This, plus the other materials, brought the cost of the loom to about $2.00. If scrap lumber is used, then a whole loom can be constructed for only the cost of the metal corner brackets, screws, and bolts. A sturdy picture frame makes a good loom also.

In order to have the loom easily portable, the size was kept at 16″x20″. But, it can be much larger and it can have legs. If a larger size than 24″x28″ is desired, then the loom should be made of hard wood at least 1″ thick and 2½″ wide. Otherwise, the frame will be too flimsy for the additional tension of a wider and longer warp.

Materials Needed

For the Frame 4 stretcher sides (or strips)—2 sides, 16″ long and 2 sides, 20″ long. These sides come from 8″ to 36″ and are prepared for joining. If scrap lumber is used for this size frame, it should be of hard wood, ¾″ thick, 1¾″ wide, and the same lengths as above.

For the Heddle Rod 2, 2½″ metal corner brackets with screws to attach to the frame.
1 wooden dowel rod at least ½″ in diameter and as long as the width of the loom.
2 wood screws with binder heads to attach the heddle rod to the corner brackets.

For the Warp-end Bar 1 wooden dowel rod at least ½″ in diameter. The length can be the same as the width of the loom or up to 4″ shorter.

For the Shed Stick 1 flat piece of wood 3″ to 4″ longer than the width of the loom, ⅜″ thick in the center, and 1½″ wide. Since it will endure stress, the wood used must be very hard and sturdy. The long edges should be sandpapered until they are rounded and smooth. No sharp edge should remain to cut the warp ends as the sheds are made.

For the Tension Stick 1 or 2 thin, flat pieces of wood or extra heavy cardboard the width of the warp.

Tools Needed Hammer, wood drill, screwdriver, saw, and sandpaper.

Steps in Construction

1. If the stretcher is used, join its four sides at right angles by inserting the projections into the ready-made grooves. Insert the triangular wooden pegs that come with the stretcher sides into the inner corners of the frame and pound in firmly. If you have difficulty keeping the frame in position and maintaining the right angle, use a brace device as shown.

If scrap lumber is used, first saw the wood into the needed lengths and widths. Sandpaper any rough edges on which the yarn might catch, and smooth the corners. Lay the two short sides *on* the long sides at the corners and attach them with wood screws that will go through two thicknesses of wood. Two or three screws at each corner will be enough to hold the frame firmly in place. You can do an even better job if you put washers under the screw heads and a nut, or binder head, where the screw exits from the back of the frame. If the screw protrudes from the nut, tape over it so that it will not scratch or mar the furniture.

Remember that you weave in just the open space between the side supports so that if you make a loom that is 16″ wide, the weaving width will be actually 12″. This is enough width to weave the projects in this book.

2. Bore two small holes on either side of the loom, four in all. The top holes should be 4½″ from the top edge and the bottom holes, 5¾″ from the top edge. These distances are based on the 20″ high loom. If you are going to make a larger loom, the bottom hole should be down about a third of the length of the entire loom.

The holes are for the screws that attach the metal corner brackets to the loom. The brackets are at right angles to the frame. Onto this, the first dowel rod is attached.

3. Place the end of the first dowel rod over the hole at the tip of the metal bracket. Mark the dowel where it touches the hole and bore a hole through the dowel end. Repeat this at the other end. Place the rod onto the brackets again and affix with the screws. Attach a binder head to the screws where they come through the rod and bracket. This is the heddle rod and in time will have string heddles attached to it.

4. Saw or file shallow notches on the top and bottom of the loom. These notches, or grooves, should be spaced ½″ apart and extended across the entire width, starting 2″ in from both edges.

5. The warp-end bar, tension sticks, and the shed stick are inserted when the warp is wound around the loom. The heddles are made at that time also.

About the Warp

The diagram of the frame loom on the opposite page illustrates how the loom should look when warped, or threaded. For complete warping instructions for the frame loom, see pages 38–39.

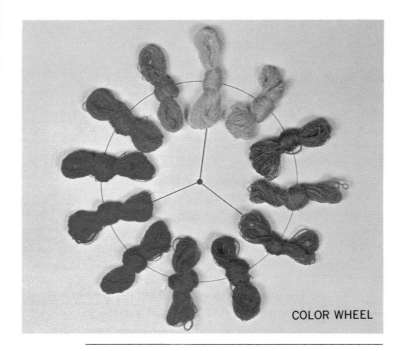

COLOR WHEEL

COLOR

Color is one of the most appealing features of weaving and, to many, one of the most challenging. A color can change according to quantity used, quality (texture or finish) of the yarn, and the surrounding colors of warp and filling.

Segments of two rugs of identical design, showing how designs are influenced by a change in color.

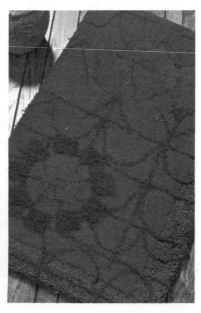

COLOR VOCABULARY

All colors have the following characteristics:
Hue The pure color and name of family in the spectrum it belongs to. Red is a pure color; pink, rose, crimson, and wine belong to the red family.
Value The amount of lightness or darkness in a hue. The hue remains the same, but with the addition of white or black the value changes. Pink is a light value of red; wine a dark value.
Intensity The brightness or dullness of a color. Again hue is retained but the closer the color comes to the pure hue, the brighter it is; the further away, the duller it is.

Colors are classified according to their positions on a color wheel as shown:

Primary The pure colors from which all others derive. Red, yellow, and blue.
Secondary The colors that lie between the primaries, made by mixing two primaries. Orange, violet, green.
Tertiary The colors made by combining adjacent primaries and secondaries. Yellow-orange, red-orange, red-violet, blue-violet, blue-green, yellow-green.
Complementary The colors opposite each other on the wheel. Red is the complement of green, blue of orange, etc. If you mix two complementary colors of equal intensity, gray results. Mixing a hue with a little of its complement dulls its intensity.
Tint Blending hue with white.
Shade Blending hue with black.
Tone Blending hue with gray (black and white).

Besides the three principal characteristics of color—hue, value, intensity—every color falls into one of seven categories—pure hue, black, white, gray, tint, shade, tone. For example, a pale blue is a mixture of a blue hue with white and is called a tint. It also has a certain amount of value and intensity depending upon the amount of white and how far the resulting color is removed from the original hue. When you look at colors, try to fit them into the correct category, to really see what makes up each color.

In choosing your colors, you will find they form a color scheme that fits into one of these harmonies:

Monochromatic Two or more values of one hue.
Analogous Combination of neighboring colors on color wheel.
Contrast Combination of complements or near-complements. Their intensity can be almost the same or vary greatly.

SOME COLOR GUIDEPOSTS

1. When deciding upon colors, consider where the finished work will be used and with what other colors it will be seen. Twist the colors together to see the effect, or wind yarn around strips of white paper to simulate the warp. Then interweave the filling colors. These tests show how colors reflect each other's hue and change character when placed together.

2. Color can be heavy, bright, light, sharp, or delicate. Reds, oranges, and yellows can be warm and exciting; blues, violets, and greens, cool and calming. White with a color makes the color look deeper and darker even though the overall effect may be light. Black gives the color a lighter and more brilliant look.

3. Neighboring colors on the wheel subtract their common color from each other. For example, in a green and turquoise combination, the green looks more like yellow-green since the blue in it combines visually with the blue in the turquoise. The same green next to lime will have a bluish green hue since the yellow in it combines with the yellow in the lime.

4. When using several colors of great intensity, the brightest will appear even brighter, and the least bright almost dull, even though it may have looked bright by itself. If you want bright colors, but not an overall bright "look," weave in enough neutral or dull colors to diminish the intensity of the bright ones.

5. In a rug, tapestry, or wall hanging an area of great darkness can be created by placing it next to a very light area. Bright areas next to dark ones make the bright, brighter; the dark, darker. Keep in mind when making stripes or plaids that equal amounts of a light or dark color make the light appear larger; the dark smaller. Warm colors also appear larger if combined with equal amounts of cool colors.

6. Complements can give very dramatic effects. When of the same intensity, they clash, but by changing the weave or by reducing the amount or intensity of one color, you get a less vibrant combination. A color and its complement, used in the right proportion, will retain that color closest to its original hue because the color does not borrow from or reflect the complement but fights with it for prominence. Neutrals also bring forth a color in its truest hue.

7. Two yarns of different hues could be combined to give the impression of a third hue. A red yarn and a blue yarn will give a purplish effect. Yarn texture will affect color. A fuzzy mohair in the same color as a gleaming smooth rayon will not look as bright as the rayon.

8. Weave structure is a factor when choosing colors. A weave that brings more of the warp or filling to the surface affects color differently than one showing equal amounts of both. A porous fabric with a low number of ends and picks per inch gives an entirely different color impression than one that is firmly and tightly constructed.

Detail of scarf (left) showing how yarn colors change when interwoven. The three swatches (right) are all woven on the same warp. The different combinations are the result of changing the filling colors and weave.

YARNS

Yarns To weavers, yarns are the raw materials of their creations. They are both a source of inspiration and limitation.

Weaving is a craft of touching as well as seeing. The way a yarn feels between your fingers guides you to use it in the proper way or to explore in new directions for different uses. You should take the time to "get to know" your yarns before you begin to weave.

One yarn can enhance another or detract from it. Textured yarns mixed together can create their own patternwork. All sorts of wonderful discoveries are possible, and when you add the heady element of color, it is easy to understand why weavers say that there is never enough time to try all the experiments they have in mind. However, all is not done with wild abandon. There are a few ground rules that, if followed, can save a lot of frustration.

Warp Yarns The first step in weaving is choosing the yarn for the warp and filling. The warp will be under tension and must be ready to take much strain and wear as the filling is woven into it. Not all yarns can be used for the warp, although just about any yarns can be used for the filling—even reeds or long grasses picked in the fields.

Even though the warp *must* be strong to withstand the weaving process, it does not necessarily have to be made of heavy or thick yarns. Some synthetic yarns are almost gossamer fine, yet are extremely strong. The properties of the yarn to be used depend on how the woven article will be used.

If a yarn is not marked for warp use and you are unsure of its strength, test to see if it breaks or frays easily. A yarn that clings together is best avoided by beginners, as extra caution and experience are needed to get a clear and wide shed.

For rugs and tapestries it is advisable to have a warp yarn that is exceptionally strong since it will undergo tremendous beating in the process of being covered. Wrapping twine and heavy string are excellent for carpet warps.

Filling Yarns Filling is also known as picks, weft, or woof. Besides weaving yarns, you can use embroidery, knitting, crocheting, and sewing yarns and threads. Do not hesitate to mix novelty yarns with plain yarns, dull with lustrous, soft furry with hard twist, and thick with very fine. The only restraint a beginner should exercise is in combining *too many* varieties of different textures or thickness in one fabric.

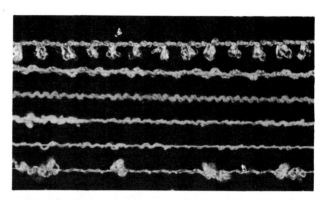

Some textured novelty yarns of various weights and strengths available to the handweaver.

Weaving with materials other than yarn. Detail of screen, woven of bark strips, wool, and square wooden beads, by Hella Skowronski. (Photograph Don Normark)

Warp yarns stand out stronger than the filling yarns if the warp is dense in the reed (*i.e.,* if there are many ends per inch). The filling will be stronger if the number of warp ends per inch is less than the filling picks per inch. A pick or shot is a single thread of filling.

A new texture or color can be achieved by twisting two dissimilar yarns or colors together in one pick.

The yarn should fit the purpose of the project. For

example, don't have scratchy or stiff yarns in apparel fabrics, blankets, or towels.

If you have doubts about how a yarn will look weave a small trial or sample swatch. The lessons learned in making these swatches are invaluable.

FIBERS

Fibers Fibers twisted together make a yarn. Longer fibers produce stronger yarns than shorter fibers.

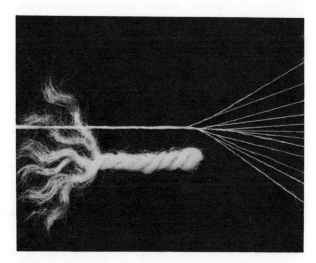

Two yarns of varying weights untwisted to show how many strands make up each ply.

Linen, cotton, wool, and silk are the most common natural fibers, and of these, linen has the least elasticity; wool the most.

Synthetics usually have less elasticity than natural fibers. Common synthetics are rayon, nylon, orlon, zefran, and fiberglass, and of these, rayon is the most used and most available to the weaver. Synthetics are found alone or in combination with natural fibers or other synthetics. Each synthetic fiber has its own properties just as a natural fiber has.

When the fibers are spun, they are twisted together to form a continuous thread or yarn of a certain size and strength. The finished strand is given a number determined by the amount of yarn it takes to make up a pound. This number, called the *count,* designates the size or thickness of the yarn. A fine

yarn has more lengths per pound, carry a higher number than a heav This is true of linen, cotton, wool a A denier system, based on weights pe used for filament silk and most synthe the reverse is true (*i.e.,* the coarser the y.ii, the higher the number; the finer the yarn, the lower the number).

If a strand of yarn is used alone, it is called a singles. When two or more single threads are twisted together, they form a ply. This is designated by two numbers. For example, a number such as 20/2 means that the yarn is made of two strands of 20 singles. The smaller number indicates the amount of strands twisted together; the larger number indicates the thickness of a single strand. Most weaving yarns are 2, 3, or 4 ply. When you are buying yarn and find no indication of yards per pound, the following table will help to determine the amount needed. The table is based on a certain number of lengths per pound of each fiber. The number varies from fiber to fiber.

Cotton,	#1 yarn	1 lb. = 840 yds.
Run Wool (unplied)	#1 yarn	1 lb. = 1600 yds.
Worsted Wool (plied)	#1 yarn	1 lb. = 560 yds.
Linen	#1 yarn	1 lb. = 300 yds.
Spun Silk	#1 yarn	1 lb. = 840 yds.

To find the number of yards for a plied yarn, divide the ply number into the yarn number and multiply the result by the correct yardage above. For example, to find the yards per pound of 20/2 cotton:

$$20 \div 2 = 10 \times 840 = 8400 \text{ yds. per lb.}$$

However, for spun silk, you have to multiply the ply and yarn numbers instead of dividing. For example, 20/2 spun silk would be calculated as follows:

$$20 \times 2 = 40, 40 \times 840 = 33,600 \text{ yds. per lb.}$$

In many blends and novelty twists, it is difficult to determine the yards per pound, and if the supplier has not noted it on the label or price sheet, I would suggest writing to him for this information.

Museum pieces are sources of color inspiration. This fragment (above) of an ancient Peruvian textile provided the color scheme for the poncho. (See page 84)

Black-eyed Susans (above) suggested the color scheme for the gold Greek bag. (See page 66) A seashore scene (below) suggested color and design for the tapestry below. (See page 70)

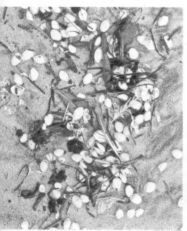

Robert Dunne, Photo Researchers

COLOR PLANNING

Nature, the greatest source of inspiration, offers limitless ideas for color schemes and patterns. Some are to be found in the spontaneous groupings of wildflowers, the graining and marbling of rocks, or the white and cream tones of seashells that have been tempered by sand and sea.

Color is not limited to field and shore; there is much in cities to inspire us in the ivy-covered bricks and weathered stones of buildings or in patterns of structural beams and the shadows they create.

Not to be overlooked are the collections of paintings and the relics of former cultures assembled in museums and the exotically colored marine and wildlife in aquariums and zoos.

As if there weren't enough in our natural surroundings to stimulate our search for ideas, we also have available beautifully colored photographs in magazines. We should study these to see how color groupings have been arranged and how designs have been balanced. Notice how the colors blend and observe the harmonious effect of one color placed against another.

One observation that I feel we can all benefit by is noticing the proportions in nature, or in a painting or photograph. There is just the right balance between the spots on a butterfly's wing and the color of the entire wing. The same is true of a painting we admire. There is just enough of each color to make the whole composition unified. To get this unity is what we should all strive for, whether we are doing a fabric, a pillow cover, a rug, or a wall hanging.

If planning colors seems a bit mystifying at first, don't be discouraged; with just a little practice you will see how easy it is. And as you become increasingly aware of the color that surrounds you, your heightened perceptions will enable you to create far more beautiful woven pieces.

Irwin L. Oakes, Photo Researchers

The colors and design for the rya rug were adapted from a natural arrangement of waterlilies in a forest pond setting. There was no attempt in the color sketch to duplicate the scene literally. Note transition of this adaptation from simple color impression to completed rug. The sketch is also a help to the weaver in selecting the proper yarn colors.

DYEING YARNS

There will be times in the course of weaving when the colors available in yarn supply houses will not please you. Or, for some reason, the yarn you want cannot be found in the color you need. This happens even though the handweaver today has a greater choice of yarns in a wider range of colors than ever before. There is no reason for you to become discouraged, however, or even to abandon that planned project. Just get ready for another adventure—dye your own yarn!

Dyeing yarn is a craft that could take several volumes to cover thoroughly. This book only hopes to skim the surface of its possibilities and to encourage you to try your hand at it. Lack of the right color is only one reason for dyeing yarns. It is also the practical approach if you want to change the color of leftover yarns or those yarns bought in wild or thoughtless moments. There are also effects and shadings you can get only by home dyeing.

It is not necessary to be surrounded by huge bubbling cauldrons in order to attain lovely results. In a small apartment kitchen the same delightful colors can come into being, and with a minimum of time and fuss. When I first decided to dye my own yarns, I set a special day apart and prepared for a long ordeal. I soon found it to be a stimulating interlude, one that I look forward to now as a period of relaxation after a hard day.

The principle of dyeing yarns can be simply outlined. The dye is mixed with hot water; into this the presoaked yarn is immersed and stirred. The dye fastens itself upon the yarn or interacts with it. Dyes are usually classified as natural or artificial and we will discuss both. Keep in mind that all yarns must be clean and the water used should be soft.

METHODS OF OBTAINING AND CHANGING COLORS

Dyeing over Unbleached or White Yarn The easiest to handle since there is no color in the yarn to affect the new one. You can get anything from a pastel to a deep shade, depending on how much dye is used. If you do not want the full intensity of color, add either a touch of gray or the complement to the dye-bath.

Dyeing over Gray or Beige Yarn A softer or grayer tone will be produced since the full intensity of the dye can not be attained.

Bleaching Dyed Yarn to Get a Lighter Color This can be done to some extent by soaking and washing dyed yarn in a detergent bath. To take out a little more color, heat the bath to a simmering point. If you want the shade still lighter, a household bleach can be used, but follow label directions carefully, especially in regard to fiber content, since too much bleach will weaken some yarns. Always rinse thoroughly after bleaching. Do not become overzealous in your efforts to lighten the color for yarn appears darker when wet. Let it dry before judging its true shade. Test a small quantity of yarn first and keep a record of the proportion of bleach or detergent to water. Even bleaching, like even dyeing, calls for complete immersion of the yarn and occasional stirring while soaking.

Changing Yarn Color by Dyeing Light or Pastel Hues a Deeper Tone Adding a color of the same family will produce a deeper shade. For example, if you have a light pink, but want a rose, dye over it with a deeper shade in its own color family. If you use a complement, or a neighboring color on the color wheel (see page 18), all manner of muted or brilliant tones can be achieved. But restrain yourself from putting in too much of the new color. A gradual buildup will produce the desired result more often than trying to hit the shade right on the mark the first time. These experiments can be tried on solid color yarns or on tweed mixtures.

Graying a Bright Color Any strong color can be grayed with a weak dye of its complement, or one of gray. Be sure that it is a *weak* dye-bath; too strong a solution will result in a mud color.

Relating Many Different Colors If you have yarn in colors that you feel do not relate, dye the whole batch in a common bath. They can be as widely separated on the color wheel as red, yellow, and blue—or of the same color family as red, rust, and orange. Choose a new color, or a dye-bath of the complement, and the yarns will emerge from the bath with a color harmony that unites them.

Ikat Dyeing, or Tie and Dye The technique known as Ikat dyeing comes to us from southeast Asia, where it was used to produce a variety of patterns. Sections of either the warp or filling can be dyed in this manner. Tie waxed cord evenly and tightly around the yarn so that no dye can penetrate to them. Tie at intervals according to the pattern desired.

Dip Dyeing The objective here is to get varied shades in the yarn. For this process, dip one end of the yarn into the dye-bath while holding the rest of it out of the solution. Then dye another section and continue doing so until the yarn is all dyed. Use either one dye-bath of the same color in intensities varying from strong to weak or several baths of different colors. If you use different colors, be careful not to overlap them or there will be muddy intervals in the yarn.

Piece Dyeing This is a way to achieve unusual color effects and shadings in the already woven cloth. Different fibers will absorb the dyes in varying degrees, and some not at all.

Dyeing a Deeper Shade or Black If your previous attempts have produced very uneven colors, or ones that you cannot use, dye them a deeper shade or black. Dyeing black over some colors, especially red, may not produce a true deep black. In this case, add a little of the complement to the dye bath. By over-dyeing black, past errors can be eliminated, and no yarn ever wasted. But, beware of this "crutch" or you will soon have a yarn bin full of home-dyed black yarn.

EQUIPMENT NEEDED

Soft Water A few drops of acetic acid or vinegar will sometimes soften hard water.

Large Enamel Pan This will be used as the dye pot. I prefer a white one so that I can see the exact color of the bath and not the reflected color of the pan. The pan should be large enough to contain sufficient water to cover the yarn without crowding it. Stainless steel and copper can also be used.

Wooden or Glass Rods and Spoon These are for lifting the yarn and stirring the bath. On one occasion I resorted to long, wooden chopsticks I had at home and found them very adequate. If you use the wooden rods, be sure to have a different one for every color. Tongs, such as the ones used for Easter eggs dyeing, are also good for lifting yarn out of the bath.

Plastic or Enamel Buckets or Pans For wetting-out, or soaking, the yarn and for rinsing after dyeing. Different pans will be needed unless you can successfully rotate both processes in the same container. You could also do both in the sink, but be sure to have a pan in which to carry the dripping yarn as you go from stove to sink.

Rubber Gloves and an Apron Dye will sometimes splatter so it is wise to wear a large cover-all apron or old clothes. The rubber gloves are necessary only if you mind having dye on your hands. Most dye will come off by scrubbing with Lava or Fels-Naptha soap, lemon juice, or weak solutions of bleaching agents.

A Glass Measuring Cup In which to mix a concentrate of the dye.

Soap Flakes For the wetting-out process that takes place before the yarn is dyed. This helps the dye to penetrate further into the yarn.

Common Salt This is used at the end to exhaust the dye-bath.

Glass Jars with Lids You should have some rather large ones in case you want to save the dye-bath and smaller ones in which to save the dye solution.

NOTE: If, after you have finished dyeing your yarns, you find you have colors that you never expected to get and don't want to dye all of them black, put them aside and plan a later project around them. No yarn need ever be thrown out or wasted. You will be surprised at the weaving ideas some unexpected color results will give you.

Be sure to keep accurate and complete records of the dye-baths. In a notebook, attach samples of yarns before and after dyeing and mark down beneath them the formula used for each shade. This will prove invaluable when you want to duplicate a shade later. If, however, in spite of your record keeping, nothing seems to approximate the color you want when you try to match it on successive days, do not be upset. Part of the fascination of home dyeing is the subtle variations of color obtained. Use this to advantage in your handweaving.

Above: Ikat-dyed tapestry by Karen Chang, in the process of being woven. Right: The completed tapestry.

Common Dye-Bath: Yarns of different colors, but of same fiber content, before and after immersion in a common dye-bath. The original colors have caused variations in the dyed colors. **Dip-Dye:** Sections of the skein were dipped in different dye-baths producing variegated shades in one skein. Care was taken not to overlap the colors which would have produced muddy intervals in the yarn. **Diluted Dye-Bath:** Two yarns of the same fiber content. Right: The yarn was dyed in a full-strength bath. Left: The yarn was dyed in the same bath, diluted.

COMMON DYE–BATH   DIP-DYE   DILUTED DYE–BATH

COMMERCIAL DYES

Commercial or artificial dyes can be bought at any five and dime store. There are also other brands that can be sent away for, and these are listed in the supply section of this book. They are all easy to handle, but the success of the project depends on following instructions carefully and in selecting the proper dye for a particular fiber. The packages usually contain an amount that will dye a whole pound of white yarn to full intensity of the color indicated. General instructions follow for the use of commercial dyes.

1. Be sure the yarn is clean. Wind it into skeins and tie loosely but securely. If tied too tightly, rings will appear where the dye could not penetrate.
2. Prepare a wetting-out bath of warm water and a small amount of soap flakes. Soak the yarn in this bath for about ten minutes, or until saturated.
3. While the yarn is soaking, have the water for the dye-bath simmering on the stove. There should be enough water in the bath to completely cover the yarn. Put the dye in the measuring cup and dissolve with hot water. This can be a paste mixture or a watery solution, depending on the dye used. Follow package directions carefully.
4. Pour some of the dye concentrate into the bath,

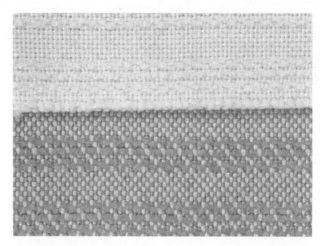

A dye-bath on yarns of same colors but of different fiber content.

A dye-bath on yarns of different colors but same fiber content.

Piece dyeing is done to change or to correct the color of a woven fabric. Place mat is shown before and after dyeing.

but in small amounts. If the yarn dries too light, you can always redye it with a stronger solution; if you add too much dye, and the yarn dries too deep, you will have the harder job of removing some of the color.

5. Take the yarn out of the wetting-out bath and squeeze dry.

6. Put the yarn into the dye-bath. Stir so that there will be even penetration. Keep at a simmering point until you have the shade you are after, or until the dye-bath is exhausted. Remember that wet yarn will appear darker than dry yarn. Read the timing instructions that come with your particular dye.

7. Add the hot water that has been simmering on the stove to the dye-bath for the next skein or color change. From one dye-bath, you can get several others. Just add hot water to replace any taken up by the preceding batches, and more dyestuff, if necessary, of the same color or a new color.

8. When using artificial dyes, it is a good idea to add a tablespoon of common salt to the dye-bath at the end of the dyeing period. This will exhaust whatever dye is left.

9. When the yarn is the color you want, lift it from the dye-bath and transfer it to the rinsing bath. Allow most of the dye to drip back into the pot.

10. Rinse the yarn in a bath only slightly cooler than the dye-bath, then progress to successively cooler baths until the water runs clear. The last bath can be quite cool.

11. After the final rinsing, squeeze the yarn—do not wring—and hang in a shaded place to dry.

12. Save any leftover dye by putting it in the large covered containers. The concentrate will go into the small containers. Be sure that all are accurately labeled.

13. During this entire process, you should be noting down amounts of dyestuff, water, etc.

NATURAL DYES

The directions listed thus far apply for the most part to artificial dyes, but there is another category of dyes obtained from natural substances such as roots, lichens, buds, leaves, flowers, berries, seeds, twigs, branches, and tree bark. The dyes from nature can be used alone or in combination with each other.

Part of the attraction of dyeing with natural substances are the excursions to the woods and fields that are made in order to gather the dyestuffs. However, if you are unable to do this, there are household items that also produce natural dyes. Among these are onion skins, coffee, tea, and cinnamon bark.

Many natural dyes change color according to the mordant used. A mordant is a substance that binds the color to the fiber through a chemical action with the dye. Mordanting controls the colors of dyes and makes them permanent. It can be done before, during, or after dyeing.

There is a little bit more uncertainty with natural dyes than with artificial ones. You should not expect to find it easy to repeat the same color at another dyeing, and it is also a game of chance to arrive at the exact color you want in the first place. Besides the variables encountered in the kitchen when we prepare the dyestuff, we must take into account that the natural sources of the dye may differ according to region and season. The soil it grows in, the length of the summer's warmth, the amount of sun and rainfall are all factors that produce differences. But don't be put off trying natural dyes. Yarns dyed in this manner have a warmth and softness of color never achieved in a commercial dye house. Their loveliness more than compensates for any difficulties you may encounter when dealing with them.

Following is a very general set of directions on how to obtain and use the natural dyestuff:

1. Gather the dyestuff. Clean of foreign matter, dry, and crush, unless it is to be used fresh. Since many natural dyestuffs are seasonal, it is best to gather them when you can, then dry and store them.

2. Put a small amount of water into an enamel bowl and steep the dyestuff from two hours to overnight.

3. After steeping, boil for half an hour to two hours.

4. Strain off liquid through cheesecloth. Save the remaining solid matter by wrapping it in several layers of cheesecloth. This can be covered with water and reboiled for about an hour.

5. Add 4 gallons of water to the dyestuff. Heat to lukewarm.

6. Add the wetted-out wool. If the mordant has already been added to the wool, the last rinsing out of the mordant should have been in water of the same temperature as the dye-bath. If the mordanting is to follow dyeing, then the yarn should be rinsed out in a lukewarm bath.

7. Bring the dye-bath to a simmer and continue simmering for the time indicated in your recipe.

8. Remove the yarn from the bath when dyeing is complete. Rinse first in a hot bath, then progress to successively cooler baths until the water runs clear.

9. Dry in the shade after squeezing out excess water.

MORDANTS

Before Dyeing Yarns

Wool should be thoroughly washed of its grease in a mild soap flake bath. If it should dry between this bath and mordanting, be sure to wet it out again. The mordant bath is a solution of 4 oz. of alum (less for lighter shades) and 1 oz. of cream of tartar to 4-4½ gals. of water. Use soft water at a warm temperature. Dissolve alum and cream of tartar first in a small amount of water, then add it to the warm water. Add the wool to the warm mordant and bring slowly to a simmer. Keep at a simmer for an hour, stirring occasionally with a glass rod. Remove from mordant, rinse thoroughly, and take to the dye-bath or dry.

Silk is mordanted the same as wool, but both *raw silk* and *spun silk* contain a waxy gum that must be removed. For raw silk, boil off the gum in a strong soap bath; for spun silk, wash it off in a warm soap bath.

Cotton, Linen, and Rayon Are Mordanted in Three Solutions

The first solution contains 4 oz. of alum and 1 oz. of washing soda to 4 gals. of water. Boil one hour and keep overnight in the mordant.

Squeeze out and put in a bath of 1 oz. tannic acid to 4½ gals. of water. Keep at a slight simmer for one hour. Cool and let stand overnight.

Remove and rinse slightly, then repeat step #1. Rinse the yarn the next day, squeeze out excess water, and put it into the dye-bath.

After Dyeing Yarns

After removing the yarn from the dye-bath, put it into a 5% solution of tannic acid to 1 gal. of water. Let it stay for thirty minutes, then remove to a new solution of 5% tartar emetic and 1 gal. of water for fifteen minutes. Rinse thoroughly and dry.

USE CAUTION WITH THE TARTAR EMETIC SINCE IT IS A POISON.

If only part of the skein is put into the mordant, it will be a different color than the rest of the skein. If you are adding a mordant to a dye-bath to deepen a color, do so sparingly—use small pinches of the mordant.

There are other mordants that can be used, such as chrome, iron sulphate, and slaked lime. The type of mordant and amount used depend on the color you are after. I have been fortunate in finding mordant supplies at my corner drugstore and supermarket. If you live in a locale where such things are not easily come by, ask your druggist to order small amounts for you.

It is well to approach natural dyeing with a feeling of experimentation. You will then be surprised and delighted with the color that results—whether or not it is the one you want.

On page 31 is a list of common plants and trees from which we can obtain many lovely shades. The rule-of-thumb ratio that I have used in the formulas for natural dyeing has been 1 lb. of dry wool to 1 lb. of the dyestuff to 4-4½ gallons of water. If you wish to dye ½ lb., or even ¼ lb., then, of course, halve or quarter the amounts of water and dry substance. More than 1-lb. lots of wool might be difficult to handle. Put in more of the dyestuff if the color comes out too weak.

As you can see, the world of dyeing—whether with artificial or natural dyes—offers unlimited fields for exploration and experimentation. We have just scratched the surface. *Do* go on and see what lies beneath it—but with this caution: Don't get so intrigued by dyeing yarns that you forget your weaving.

NATURAL DYE SOURCES

Various natural dye sources and the colors obtained from them. The color on the left is full strength and the tint on the right is half strength.

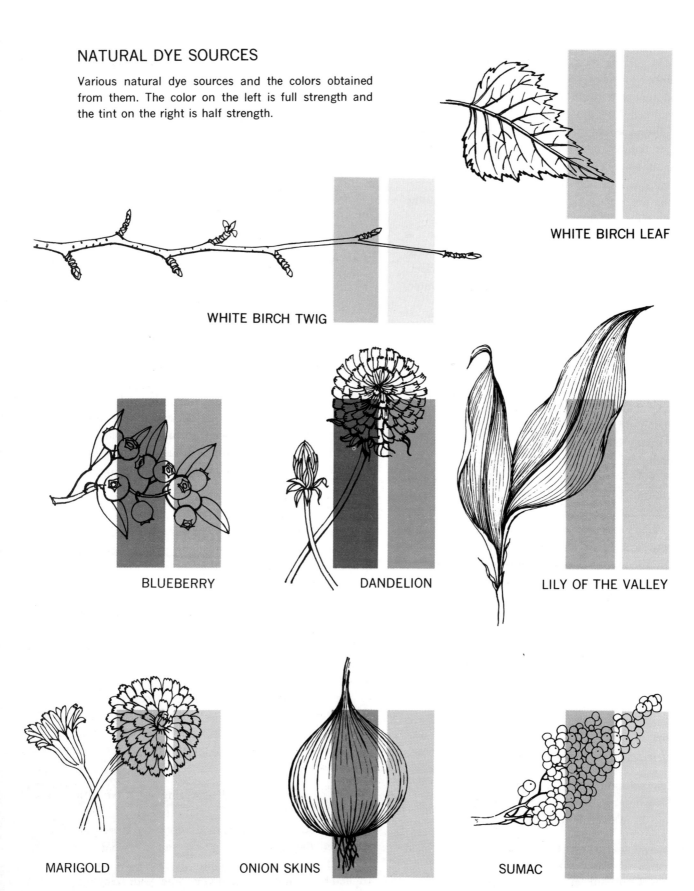

WHITE BIRCH LEAF

WHITE BIRCH TWIG

BLUEBERRY

DANDELION

LILY OF THE VALLEY

MARIGOLD

ONION SKINS

SUMAC

DYESTUFF	SOURCE	COLOR	MORDANT	MISCELLANEOUS NOTES
ALDER	BARK, LEAVES BARK	BLACK BROWN	IRON SULPHATE	
AZALEA	LEAVES LEAVES	DARK GRAY BROWNISH RED	WEAK IRON SULPHATE SLAKED LIME	PICK LEAVES IN LATE FALL.
BAYBERRY	LEAVES	GRAYISH GREEN	ALUM	PICK LEAVES IN SUMMER.
BLACKBERRY	YOUNG SHOOTS	LIGHT GRAY TO BLACK	ALUM	ADD IRON SULPHATE TO DEEPEN COLOR.
BLACK WALNUT	GREEN OUTER HUSKS	DARK BROWN TO BLACK	NO MORDANT NEEDED, BUT SOAK SHELLS WELL.	PICK HUSKS WHILE GREEN, REMOVE BY POUNDING WITH HAMMER.*
BLUEBERRY	BERRY	BLUE TO PURPLE	ALUM	
DANDELION	ROOTS WHOLE PLANT	PURPLE MAGENTA	NO MORDANT NEEDED	
ELDERBERRY	BERRY BERRY BERRY LEAVES	BLUE LILAC VIOLET TO PURPLE GREEN	SALT ALUM CHROME ALUM	CRUSH BERRIES BEFORE SOAKING DEPTH OF COLOR DEPENDS ON AMOUNT USED AND LENGTH OF BOILING.
GOLDENROD	FLOWER	YELLOW-TAN OLD GOLD	ALUM CHROME	PICK WHEN FLOWERS ARE JUST ABOUT TO BLOOM.
LILY-OF-THE- VALLEY	LEAVES	LIME GREENY GOLD	CHROME CHROME	PICK IN SPRING. PICK IN FALL.
MARIGOLD	FLOWER	YELLOW TO GOLD	ALUM	ADD A FEW WALNUT HUSKS FOR A DEEPER TONE.
MAPLE	BARK BARK	GRAY TO PURPLE OLIVE	IRON SULPHATE ALUM	
NETTLE	WHOLE PLANT	GREENISH YELLOW	ALUM	WEAR GLOVES WHEN PICKING OR AN ITCHY RASH WILL DEVELOP.
ONION	DRIED SKINS FROM COMMON COOKING ONION	GOLDEN YELLOW BURNT ORANGE BRASS YELLOW OLIVE GREEN	ALUM ALUM WITH TIN CHROME ALUM WITH IRON SULPHATE	MORDANT WOOL FIRST WITH ALUM.
POMEGRANATE	HARD OUTER SKIN	YELLOW BROWN VIOLET BLUE	ALUM VERY WEAK IRON SULPHATE SOLUTION ABOVE SOLUTION PLUS ASH EXTRACT	
PRIVET	BERRIES BERRIES AND LEAVES LEAVES AND BRANCH TIPS	BLUE, BLUE GREEN GREEN YELLOW GOLD	ALUM AND SALT ALUM ALUM AND CREAM OF TARTAR CHROME	ADD YARN WHEN CRUSHED BERRIES ARE BOILING.
SAFFRON	FLOWERS OR POWDER FROM GROCERY	YELLOW	ALUM	
SUMAC	BERRIES LEAVES, TWIGS	YELLOWISH TAN TO GRAY BROWN TO BLACK	ALUM AND IRON SULPHATE NO MORDANT NEEDED	PICK WHEN FULLY RIPE, CRUSH FRUIT BEFORE OVERNIGHT SOAKING. ADD IRON SULPHATE AFTER DYE.
WHITE BIRCH	LEAVES TWIGS INNER BARK	YELLOW YELLOWISH GREEN BROWN	ALUM ALUM NO MORDANT NEEDED.	LONGER BOILING WILL PRODUCE A DEEPER YELLOW. BREAK BARK INTO SMALL BITS BEFORE SOAKING.

*USE RUBBER GLOVES, AS DYE WILL STAIN. FOR DARK BROWNS, ADD IRON SULPHATE.
FOR BLACK, ADD ALSO A HANDFUL SUMAC BERRIES. LEAVE OVERNIGHT IN DYE-BATH.

WARPING

Warping is part of the process known as dressing the loom, the object being to get the calculated number of warp ends in the right arrangement and of the same length and tension. Warp ends is the term used when referring to the individual lengths or pieces of warp.

Warping is a prelude to weaving. A well-made warp will make the hours spent at the actual weaving that much more enjoyable. At first, warping will require patience from you. But, after enough warps have been put on, your gestures in warp-making will become instinctive and rhythmic, and you will find this as relaxing and enjoyable as weaving itself.

TO PREPARE YARN FOR WARPING

When making the warp by any of the methods for floor and table looms, it is necessary to have the yarn in skeins, cones, or spools. These have to be on a fixture that allows the yarn to revolve off smoothly as it is needed for the warp. Spools are usually put on spool racks, cones on yarn holders, and skeins on swifts. If these are not available, you can make substitutes. A yarn holder that will hold spools or cones can be made by hammering nails, about 4″ to 5″ long, through a piece of sturdy wood. The nails should be spaced about 6″ apart. Spools or balls of yarn can be put into boxes with high sides so that they will not tumble out as the yarn is revolved off.

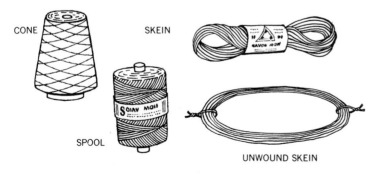

CONE   SKEIN   SPOOL   UNWOUND SKEIN

Yarns are packaged for sale in several ways, the most common of which are shown above.

Skeins can be placed around chairs. However, this method does not allow for the rapid flow of yarn.

CALCULATIONS

To arrive at the number of warp ends needed, you must decide how wide you want your woven piece to be and how heavy, or dense. The density of a fabric is determined by the number of warp ends per inch, or sett. A good formula to follow is:

sett × width = total number of ends.

For example:

sett of 10 ends per inch x width of 10″ = 100 warp ends.

To the total number of ends should be added an additional amount to compensate for the pulling in at the selvedges of the warp by the filling. A general rule of thumb is to add 1″ for every 10″ of finished width. The total number of ends in the above example is now 110. Professionally, this is calculated according to fiber content and resiliency of the yarn.

The second calculation is to determine the length of the warp ends that will be put on the loom so that your finished fabric will be the length you want. The formula for this is:

finished length
+ loom allowance
+ take up
= dressed length

Loom allowance is the amount wasted in putting the warp on the loom; also, it is the amount remaining on the loom, in and behind the harnesses, that cannot be woven off. For a floor loom allow 1 to 1¼ yds., and for a table loom, ½ yd.

The warp is under tension while it is being woven, but this tension is released as soon as the fabric is taken from the loom. In order to compensate for the difference between the tense and the released states, we must add the take up.

The take up is literally the yarn taken up in the interweaving process as the filling goes over and under the warp. Various fibers have various take ups, such as:

wool	6″ per yd.
linen	3″ per yd.
mixed yarn	4″ to 5″ per yd.

An example of the above formula follows—the problem being how much warp is needed if a 5-yd. piece of wool and silk is to be woven. It will be woven on a floor loom.

finished length	5 yds.
+ loom allowance	1 yd.
+ take up	5″ per yd.
	(or 25″)
= dressed length	6 yds., 25″
	(which we call 6¾ yds.)

The calculations for the total number of ends apply to all looms, but the calculations for the length apply only to floor and table looms. When working on the frame loom, you are limited to a warp twice the length of the loom.

WARPING METHOD #1—USING A WARPING REEL

A warping reel or drum is one method used to prepare the warp for a floor or table loom. In the most common of reels, there is ½ yd. between each side dowel. A complete trip around the reel would then be 2 yds.

Always hold the yarn taut while warping and maintain even tension throughout the whole warping operation.

Start the warp at the bottom of the reel by tying the yarn to the peg on the bottom horizontal bar. There is also a horizontal bar at the top around whose pegs the *cross* is formed. These bars may be shifted from one side of the reel to another in order to get the desired length of warp.

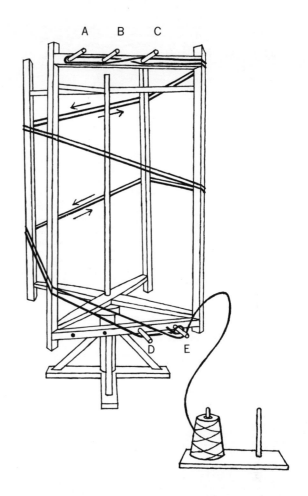

Warping method #1. Preparing the warp on a warping reel, or drum. Here the yarn is fed from a cone on a holder, onto the warping reel. Note the two crosses, one at the top and one at the bottom. Only one cross is necessary, but two are recommended for the beginner in the event that one cross is lost.

To make the warp (with crosses at both top and bottom horizontal bars), secure the beginning end at E with a loop knot around the peg. Go under D and up and around as many times as necessary for the desired length. Go under C and over B and A. You have now made one warp end, but *do not* cut the end. Continue by going under A and B and over C, return down and around to D, then over D and back under E. You are now beginning the third warp end. Procced in this manner until the total number of warp ends is reached. If it is an even number, tie and cut off at E. If it is an odd number, tie and cut off at A.

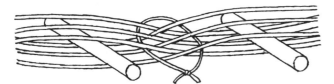

Closeup of cross tied before it is chained off the reel.

The cross that is formed on the upper horizontal bar is also called a lease. Its function is to keep the warp ends in order until the warp is completely threaded through the loom. It is possible to make a second cross on the bottom horizontal bar. This is advisable for beginners so that if one cross is lost, there will be the other one to keep the threads from tangling.

Before you take the warp off the reel, tie the cross in a contrasting color yarn so that it will not be lost in its transference to the loom. Also, at every

yard, tie the contrasting yarn around the entire group of warp threads. This is called a choke and keeps the yarns from tangling while the chain is being made and while the warp is being prepared on the loom.

CHAINING

In order to conveniently carry the warp from the reel to the loom, the length of the warp is reduced by chaining it. The chain is similar to a crochet chain, and the hand is used like a crochet hook in making it. For those unfamiliar with crocheting, the following illustrations explain the technique:

Flip the end of the warp over the hand so that it forms a loop. Pull the warp through the loop until it forms another loop. Through this loop repeat the same procedure—and so on, until the whole warp

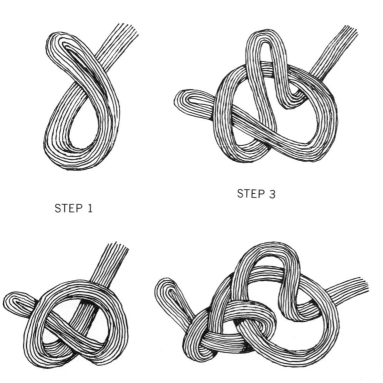

STEP 1

STEP 3

STEP 2

STEP 4

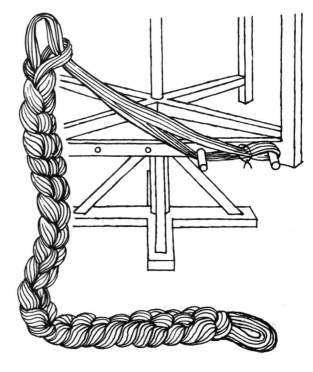

The chained warp ready to be taken to the loom from the warping reel.

is chained off. Do not pull the last loop completely through, or you will lock the chain so that it cannot be unchained later on the loom.

WARPING METHOD #2—USING A WARPING BOARD

This is an alternate method of warping for the floor or table loom. The board can be placed on a table or hung from a wall. A common size for the warping board is ½ yd. by 1 yd.

After the warp has been determined, measure it off on the board. For example, a 4-yd. warp could start at A, go *over* the peg at B, around at C and over to D, back and around at D to E, around the side at E, up to F, over F and G and under and over H. This is the route of one 4-yd. warp end. The warp is continued by returning under G, over F down to E across to D, back across the board to C, across and under B, and up and around A. This is now the beginning of the third warp end.

Continue for the needed number. Then tie the crosses and the chokes, chain and remove to the loom as explained in warping method #1.

NOTE: If you should find it difficult to keep count of the warp ends, mark off every group of 20 with a loose loop of contrasting yarn.

Alternate Methods of Warping

If you have no warping reel or board, methods can be improvised that will do the job just as well. The important points to remember are always to maintain even tension and to have a cross.

1. Three pegs driven into the ground out-of-doors. Peg A and peg C are placed as far apart as the length of the desired warp. The cross is formed between pegs A and B.
2. Kitchen chairs. These must be weighted down so that they will not shift during the warping operation. Avoid those with ornamental knobs, otherwise you will find it difficult to pull off the warp when you are through. The cross can be formed between the chairs, or made around broom handles or dowel rods at the sides of chairs.
3. Tables turned upside down or bedposts can also be used.

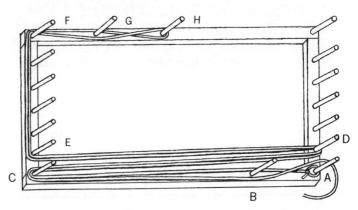

Warping method #2. Preparing the warp on a warping board.

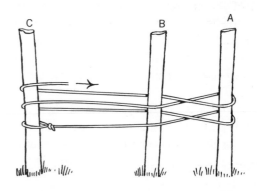

Alternate methods of warping. 1. Three pegs driven into the ground. 2. Weighted chairs used as a warping device.

BEAMING AND THREADING THE LOOM

After the chained warp has been taken to the loom, it must be rolled (beamed) onto the warp beam, threaded (draw-in) through the heddles, and threaded (sleyed) through the reed. One way of doing this is the back-to-front method. This means we will roll the warp onto the warp beam and thread from the back of the loom to the front.

1. Attach the warp to the warp beam by slipping the back apron bar through the loop formed by the warp near the cross.

2. Insert the lease rods into the warp on either side of the cross. One rod goes in back of where the threads cross and the other rod goes in front. Lease rods are usually included with the purchase of a loom. If they are not included with your loom, you can use any smooth, flat, thin rods the correct width of the loom.

3. Tie the lease rods together and then to a cord running from the castle to the back beam. They will maintain the cross while the warp is being beamed and may be removed when the sleying is finished.

4. Cut the contrasting yarn that holds the cross and spread the warp evenly to the width it is to be woven. A raddle or spreader may be used.

5. Maintain the warp under tension while it is being wound onto the warp beam. It would be best for a beginner to have a friend help so that while one holds the tension and combs the warp, the other can wind the warp beam. However, if this is not possible, then hold the warp over the castle as you wind, or bring the warp over the breast beam and attach weights to maintain the tension.

6. Stop every foot or more to shake out the warp gently and comb it with your fingers. This is done to prevent the ends from tangling and to catch any ends that may have slipped from tension.

7. Heavy paper or smooth sticks should be inserted between layers of the warp ends while beaming so that the warp will always have a smooth surface on which to maintain its tension.

8. The beaming is finished when there are only 12″ of warp left in front of the first harness. Cut the loop at this end of the warp and begin the drawing-in.

9. If the beater can be disassembled, do so, for then

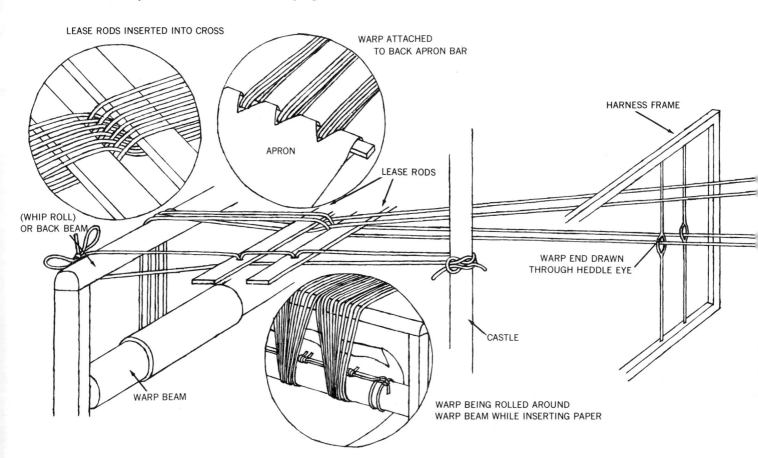

LEASE RODS INSERTED INTO CROSS

WARP ATTACHED TO BACK APRON BAR

APRON

LEASE RODS

HARNESS FRAME

(WHIP ROLL) OR BACK BEAM

WARP END DRAWN THROUGH HEDDLE EYE

CASTLE

WARP BEAM

WARP BEING ROLLED AROUND WARP BEAM WHILE INSERTING PAPER

there will be no obstruction between you and the heddles while you are threading them.

10. Place the heddles you will be using in the center of each harness. Tie off the remaining heddles on each side.

11. With a reed hook, pull the warp end through the heddle eye, from back to front. Take the yarn in consecutive order from right to left, from the lease rod nearest to the back harness. One end will come from *over* the lease rod and the other from *under*.

12. The warp ends are drawn in according to a warp plan, or drawing-in draft (see chapter on Drafting), which tells the harness number of the heddle to be threaded. The harness facing the weaver is harness number 1 and the harness facing the back beam, harness number 4 (in a 4-harness loom).

13. Check every 20 to 30 ends to see that the drawing-in is correct. Then tie the ends in a slipknot so that they will not pull out accidentally.

14. Find the center of the reed and measure the width of your warp so that it is evenly spaced on each side of the center mark.

15. Sley the warp ends through the dents in the reed according to the number that must go in each dent. The projects to follow will indicate the number of ends per dent. Sley from right to left with the reed either in the beater or lying flat and supported by rods on the side. If in the former position, sley from back to front. If in the latter positions, sley from the top down. Be sure to take the warp ends in order so that they do not cross and thus prevent a clear shed from forming. Check and tie slipknots.

16. Tie a bundle, or grouping, of warp ends to the front apron bar. This should be about the thickness of a forefinger. First tie a group to the center of the apron bar, then tie successive groups to the right and left of the center. All the groups should be tied with a single knot, as shown in diagram. Go over the groups from right to left and pull up on the knotted ends to adjust the tension. Pass your hand lightly over the warp at the back of the loom and if you feel any loosening of tension, pull up on these warp ends in the groups. Adjust the tension in the knots a third time and double knot the groups to ensure that the ends do not slip out while being woven.

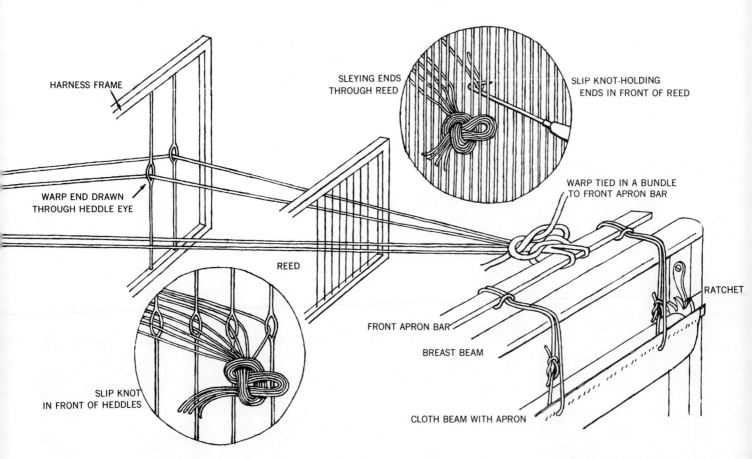

HARNESS FRAME

SLEYING ENDS THROUGH REED

SLIP KNOT-HOLDING ENDS IN FRONT OF REED

WARP END DRAWN THROUGH HEDDLE EYE

WARP TIED IN A BUNDLE TO FRONT APRON BAR

REED

SLIP KNOT IN FRONT OF HEDDLES

FRONT APRON BAR

BREAST BEAM

RATCHET

CLOTH BEAM WITH APRON

WARPING THE FRAME LOOM

The warp is made directly on the frame loom. No warping reel or board is required, nor is a cross, since the ends are put in position for weaving as the warp is being wound onto the loom. In this frame loom the warp is twice the length of the loom and can be revolved around it as the weaving progresses.

Even warp tension should always be maintained. but the ends do *not* need to be overly tight. If you find tension slackening as you are winding the warp around the loom, tug on the yarn until you find that all feels even again.

WARPING INSTRUCTIONS

1. Temporarily tape or tie the warp-end bar on the back of the loom. This is a precautionary measure to keep the bar from shifting at the beginning of warping.
2. With tape or pencil indicate the sett marks where you want the warp to begin and end. The warp ends must be spaced, while winding the warp, between every ½″ sett mark at the required number of ends per inch. For example, if you are using a sett of 10 ends per inch, one warp end goes in the notch and four between each notch. Selvedge ends are counted two as one.
3. Before warping begins, tension sticks should be taped to the front of the loom at top and bottom. They are removed as the weaving progresses and the take-up tightens the warp.
4. Wind the warp yarn into a large bobbin, it can then be held in your hand, greatly facilitating going around the warp-end bar.
5. Unscrew the heddle rod while warping.
6. Tie the warp yarn around the warp-end bar at a point directly over the beginning sett mark.
7. Take the yarn down and around to the front of the loom, up to the top and over, down to the warp-end bar, around it and *back* to the top of the loom. Go down the front, under the bottom frame, up to the warp-end bar, around it and *back* to the bottom. Continue in this manner until the required number of ends have been warped.
8. After bringing the yarn around the warp-end

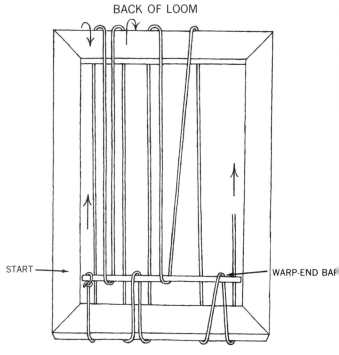

BACK OF LOOM

START →   WARP-END BAR

The frame loom is warped from the back. After going around the warp-end bar, the warp always returns in the direction from which it came.

bar, return it in the direction from which it came in order for the warp to revolve around the loom. The yarns around the warp-end bar should look like the above drawing.
9. Tie the last end to the warp-end bar and cut it free of the bobbin. Remove tape holding the warp-end bar in place. Rescrew the heddle rod.

ARRANGEMENT FOR TWO SHEDS

The warp is complete; now we must make an arrangement that will give us the two sheds.

First Shed The shed stick is used to make the first shed. Insert it at the right, above the heddle rod, and weave it *under* the *odd*-numbered ends and *over* the *even*-numbered ones. When all the ends are either over or under the shed stick, turn the stick on its edge at a right angle to the warp and check if your first shed is correct. Remember that the selvedge ends are counted two as one.
Second Shed Heddles are made for the second shed. You will need strong linen cord, preferably in a natural color, and a blunt-edged tapestry needle.

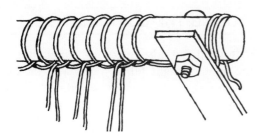

Closeup of heddle bar with string heddles attached through loops of heddle spacer.

1. Take a piece of linen cord 2 yds. long and tie one end to the heddle rod on the right side of the loom, around the screw. Move ½″ to the left and go over the rod with the cord, meanwhile holding a portion of the cord at the bottom of the rod. This forms a loop through which the cord goes after it circles the rod. This is called a half-hitch and is repeated over the entire rod at approximately ⅛″ intervals. At the other end, tie the cord around the left screw.

2. Cut as many 10″ pieces of linen cord as there are even-numbered warp ends. These 10″ pieces will become your actual heddles. Insert a piece of white paper between the back and front of the warp to aid you in seeing and picking up the warp ends.

3. Slip the 10″ pieces of linen *under* the *even-numbered* warp ends. Using the needle, insert the linen thread into the loop of the heddle cord that is directly above the warp end you are working with. Double-knot the ends of the linen cord and the heddle is complete.

It is not necessary to put on completely new heddles for your next warp. The heddles are still usable if they are long enough to give a good shed when pulled on. All that is needed is to cut the knot, loop under the new warp end, and retie. When the heddles become too short to manipulate, cut off and put new ones on. The heddle cord at all times stays in place on the heddle rod.

THE CHAIN SPACER

The last thing to be done before we start weaving is to make a chain spacer at the bottom of the warp where the weaving will begin. This serves the triple function of spacing the warp evenly,

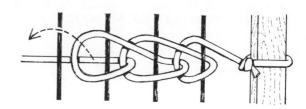

Chain spacer, the length of thread that is chained around and between the warp ends to separate them.

keeping the ends in order, and giving a firm starting edge for the first row of filling.

Steps to Follow:

1. The chain spacer should be placed so that there is enough unwoven warp between it and the warp-end bar to make a fringe, braid, or for any other method of finishing off. If the warp-end bar is so far up on the back of the loom as to cause too much unwoven warp to remain at the beginning of the piece, push the bar down towards the bottom.

2. Cut 1 yd. of the same linen cord that was used for the heddles.

3. Tie it around the right side of the frame as shown.

4. Draw the long end of the cord from under the top warp, then pull enough of it up between the first and second ends to form a small loop. The chain is really a series of loops as in crochet and some weavers even use a crochet hook in making it.

5. With thumb and forefinger, go through this loop to the right and form another loop to the right of the first end. Always pull tightly on the new loop in the right hand so that all of the slack in the chain is drawn out and the finished loops are tightly and evenly spaced.

6. Pick up yet another loop between the second and third ends and pull through the held loop. Tighten.

7. Through this loop, pull the one formed between the third and fourth ends. This is continued until all the warp ends are enclosed in loops.

8. Pull the cord through the last loop, on the left side of the warp, and this will lock the chain.

9. Tie the cord to the left side of the frame. Adjust the tie on the right side of the frame so that the warp is pulled out slightly wider than the intended width.

PREPARING THE FILLING

Once the loom is ready, we have only to prepare the filling before weaving can begin.

In order to do this, the yarn must be unwound from whatever holds it—spool, cone, or skein—and, in small amounts, put on shuttles. These are implements designed to carry the filling through the open shed from one side of the loom to the other. Shuttles come in various forms, and the one you use will depend on the width of the shed opening and the weight of the yarn.

USING THE STICK SHUTTLE

The stick shuttle is long and flat and can be easily made at home out of wood or heavy cardboard. It varies in length from 9″ to 22″. This shuttle carries heavy filling yarns or rags and is used on looms that give only narrow shed openings.

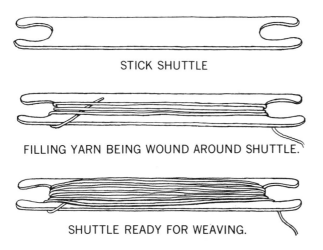

STICK SHUTTLE

FILLING YARN BEING WOUND AROUND SHUTTLE.

SHUTTLE READY FOR WEAVING.

To put the yarn on the stick shuttle, loop one end of the yarn around an arm of the shuttle and then wind a substantial amount around its length. The end result should resemble the drawing above. Do not wind on too much yarn or else it will be difficult to get the shuttle through the shed. Also broken warp ends may result if the filling yarn brushes either the top or bottom of the shed as the shuttle continually passes back and forth.

USING THE BOAT SHUTTLE

The boat shuttle is also made of wood, but it is used for lighter-weight filling yarns and on looms giving larger sheds. Since this shuttle is made so that it can be thrown from one side of the shed to the other, it is what we use when weaving wide fabrics. Boat shuttles come in a variety of types and sizes. Some come equipped with rollers on the bottom which make them glide through the shed even faster.

The boat shuttle has a steel pin in its center section which holds a removable bobbin, or quill. The filling yarn is wound around the bobbin, which is then slipped onto the pin with the starting end of the filling yarn threaded through the hole on one side of the shuttle. This hole always faces the weaver as the shuttle travels through the shed.

Most shuttles come with at least one bobbin, usually of plastic or cardboard. Extra ones can be made by rolling an oval-cut piece of heavy paper to the diameter and length of the bobbin needed. The paper must be sturdy or the bobbin will buckle in the center.

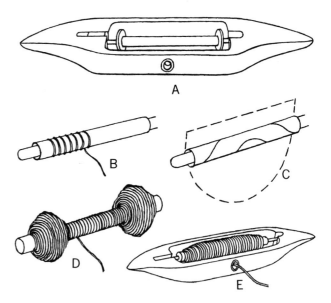

A. Boat shuttle with empty bobbin. B. A paper quill can be used as an extra bobbin. C. To make a quill, roll an oval piece of heavy paper and cut to the width and length needed. D. Proper way of winding filling yarn around quill. E. Boat shuttle with quill completely wound.

WINDING THE BOBBIN FOR THE BOAT SHUTTLE

The filling yarn is wound by hand onto the bobbin or by electric or hand bobbin winders. Many clever weavers have made bobbin winders at home by inserting a steel rod into a small electric motor (such as in a portable mixer, sewing machine, or drill).

In order to have the yarn wound on correctly, the two ends of the bobbin are built up first and the center last. If the reverse were done, the yarn could not flow off easily during weaving. It is important to have bobbins tightly wound, for if they are not, the yarn will roll off at the ends and become tangled around the shuttle pin.

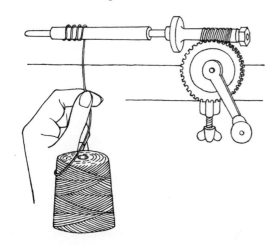

Winding the filling yarn from cone to bobbin on a hand bobbin winder.

OTHER SHUTTLES

For weaving on upright looms or on frame looms, the filling carrier should be small so that when it hangs from the weaving it will not pull at the filling. *Gobelin bobbins* (its point is used to beat down the filling) and *Aubusson flutes* are of this type. A very small cardboard shuttle, or a knitting bobbin, are also practical. The use of the latter would be limited to an occasional color since it holds only a small amount of yarn. The cardboard shuttle must have a slot on its edge in which to insert the yarn so that it won't unwind when the shuttle hangs idle by the side of the loom.

MAKING THE BUTTERFLY

On the frame loom, a butterfly of yarn can be used instead of a shuttle. A butterfly is an arrangement, or bundle, of filling yarn without a holder and is made by winding the yarn around the fingers in a figure 8. Butterflies are most often used in making the pile on rugs. They are flexible and can easily go over and under warp ends and around a gauge which is used for making the rug pile knot.

Butterflies are made on the palm of the hand. The starting end of the yarn, as it comes from the skein or spool, is clasped between two fingers. The yarn is then brought in back of and around the thumb and around the little finger from back to front. On its return trip to the thumb, the yarn should cross in the center; this will keep it in order and free from tangles. When a suitable amount is thus wound, cut the yarn at its source and wind this loose end around the center of the butterfly, half-hitching it twice so that it will not become undone. The other loose end, which is being held by the little finger, is the pulling end which releases the yarn for use.

NOTE: Whether you are making butterflies or bobbins, do not be misled into thinking that if you make extra large ones, you will have to make less of them and thereby save yourself time. Outsize butterflies or bobbins are difficult to manipulate. They get caught in the warp, which could lead to broken ends, or they get knotted and tangled within themselves. This only results in a frayed temper and a loss of time.

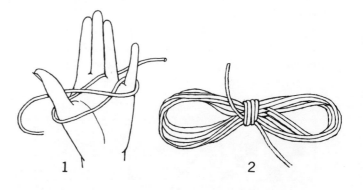

(1) Making a butterfly by winding the yarn around the fingers in a figure eight. (2) The completed butterfly.

DRAFTING WEAVES

Weaves are the patterns we achieve in the cloth through an interaction between the way the warp is threaded through the heddles and the order in which the harnesses are raised or lowered. In order for weavers to explain concisely and quickly what the weave will look like, how to thread the loom for a particular weave, and what levers or treadles to press, they use a shorthand language called drafting.

For you to understand weaving fully and get the most enjoyment and fulfillment from it, you should try to read a draft, write one, and ultimately design one.

UNDERSTANDING DRAFTING

In order to learn this shorthand language, you will need paper that is marked off into a number of small squares per inch. Called graph paper, it comes in various sizes. I have found either the 8x8 size (8 squares to the inch) or the 10x10 (10 squares to the inch) to be the easiest on the eyes. You can also make your own graph paper by simply drawing lines that cross at right angles.

Whatever the size of the paper, it is important to keep in mind that a number of blocks on paper will equal the same number of warp ends even though they may not both equal an inch.

In most cases, the graph paper weave will be larger than the actual woven weave, and it is up to the weaver to make the mental adjustment between the paper and the cloth. This ability, to visualize the weave on paper, to plan it, and to avoid mistakes in the pattern, is important to strive for while learning drafting.

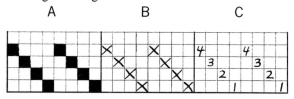

Three ways to write a drawing-in draft, or warp plan. A-Squares filled in. B-Squares X'ed in. C-Squares numbered.

When I first learned to draft in school, I naively believed there was only one way to write a draft. I have learned since that there are almost as many ways as there are weavers. However, the three methods illustrated, A, B, and C, are the ones generally used in weaving books and manuals.

TYPES OF DRAFTS

There Are Three Kinds of Drafts

Weave Draft Indicates the pattern of the weave.
Warp Plan Indicates how the loom should be threaded. Also called drawing-in draft or threading draft.
Chain Draft Indicates the order in which harnesses are raised.

When the harnesses move to give us a shed, the ends that are threaded through the heddles on these harnesses are raised. The shuttle flies through with the filling thread, the shed is changed, and another set of ends is raised. As this series of steps is repeated, a pattern comes into being—the pattern planned by you beforehand and achieved by working the treadles or levers. This is called a *"loom-controlled"* weave.

When you work at a frame loom or a 2-harness loom, both of which give only 2 sheds, you can change your fabric by laying in filling yarn in a design or by winding knots around the warp ends. These and other such techniques where the ends are picked up individually or in groups are *"finger-manipulated"* weaves and usually are not indicated on drafts except when planning an overall design.

WEAVE DRAFT AND WEAVES

The Three Basic Weaves Are: Plain, Twill, Satin

From these, all weaves are derived. By combining parts of the basic weaves, or by combining two entire basic weaves, completely new patterns can evolve. This is the exciting part of weaving, so take the time to experiment with some combinations and see what interesting and beautiful patterns you can create.

PLAIN WEAVE

Of the loom-controlled weaves, the most basic is the *plain weave,* commonly called the *tabby weave.* We come upon this weave everyday in handkerchiefs, ginghams, taffeta fabrics, and bed linens.

Plain weave is like darning. The filling goes over one warp end and under one and repeats across the width of the fabric. In the next row the filling alternates and goes under the end it had gone over and over the end it had gone under. The third row repeats the first and so we realize that this weave repeats on two filling picks. (For "pick," see glossary.)

The progression of a weave from draft to finished cloth.

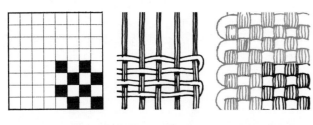

1 WEAVE DRAFT   2 ON THE LOOM   3 FINISHED CLOTH

If we look at the weave draft above, we see that end #3 is in the same position as end #1 and end #4 is in the same position as end #2. Therefore, we know the plain weave repeats every two ends. As can be seen on graph paper, a draft is an exact reproduction of what happens to the weave on the loom.

NOTE: the horizontal spaces in a *weave draft* represent the filling and the vertical spaces, the warp.

When a square is blocked in, or xed in, the filling thread goes under the warp end. If the square is blank, the filling goes over the warp end.

Plain weave can be made on a 4-, 8-, or even a 16-harness loom as long as all odd ends are always raised on one shed and all even ends are always raised on the other shed. Only the plain weave can be done easily on a frame loom or a 2-harness loom since there are just two shed possibilities.

VARIATIONS ON THE PLAIN WEAVE

Vertical Stripes Different colors in the warp.

Horizontal Stripes Different colors in the filling.

Irregular Sleying Wide spaces between some ends or groups of ends crammed together.

Varied Textures Textured yarn in warp or filling, or both.

Filling Predominate Fabric Filling completely or almost completely covers the warp. Tapestry weave is an example of this. There are fewer ends than picks per inch.

Irregular Threading Pattern This is explained in the threading section on page 47.

Modified Basket Weave Put two picks of filling instead of one in every shed.

Finger-manipulated Weaves

If you want more changes in pattern by way of more sheds, then you will need a loom that provides more sheds. For a beginner, a 4-harness loom offers more than enough possibilities for exploration, so we will limit our discussion to this. Keep in mind that whatever is possible on a 4-harness loom is also possible on 8, 12, or 16 harnesses.

TWILL WEAVE

The second basic weave, the twill, is very popular and has many variations. An even-balanced weave is produced when there is an equal number of picks and warp ends per inch. The simple diagonal effect in the twill weave makes it especially desirable for suiting and other apparel fabrics.

This weave repeats on 4 ends and 4 picks and should be made on a 4-harness loom. A balanced twill (two harnesses up and two down) is written $\frac{2}{2}$. Twills run either to the right or to the left; I have concentrated on the left-handed twills in this book.

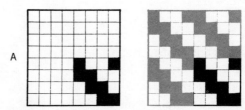

Left-handed twill—A one repeat, B two repeats in warp and filling.

VARIATIONS ON TWILL WEAVE

Filling-faced Twill
The warp is almost completely covered. It is written $\frac{1}{3}$.
2 repeats.

Warp-faced Twill
The filling is almost completely covered. It is written $\frac{3}{1}$.
2 repeats.

Broken Twill
The same weave but not woven in consecutive order.
The diagonal line of the weave is "broken" so as to achieve a textured all-over effect. 2 repeats.

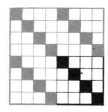

Reverse Twill
A zigzag line is formed when the weave is reversed at the end of 4 picks and runs to the right for 2 picks. 2 repeats.

In addition to these variations, completely different looks can be given to the twill weave by a multi-colored warp and filling and the use of textured yarns. There are countless other variations possible in the weave itself, diamond patterns, triangular patterns—this is an area where you can experiment with much satisfaction.

SATIN WEAVE

If you want a cloth with a smooth, lustrous surface, the satin weave is the answer to your search. This is the third basic weave and in order for it to be a "true" satin, it needs at least 5 harnesses for one repeat. However, a mock, or irregular, satin can be constructed on a 4-harness loom. The one drafted below, in 2 repeats, is called a "crowfoot" weave.

CROWFOOT SATIN

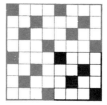

A satin weave is usually used when you wish to bring either the warp or the filling to the surface without having a set pattern to the weave. The crowfoot weave above would bring up the filling and hide most of the warp. If you wish to do the reverse, the weave would appear as shown below.

SOME COMMON WEAVES AND DRAFTS FOR A 4-HARNESS LOOM

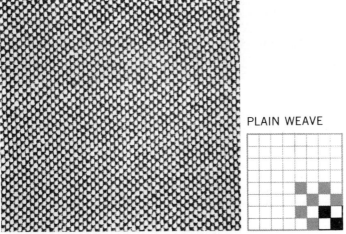

PLAIN WEAVE

1. Plain weave draft shows two repeats in filling and in warp.

MODIFIED BASKET WEAVE

2. Modified basket weave. Weave draft shows two repeats in warp and filling.

TWILL WEAVE

3. Left-handed twill weave. Weave draft shows two repeats in warp and filling.

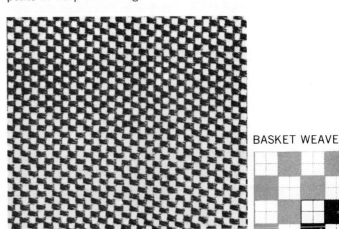

BASKET WEAVE

4. Basket weave. Weave draft shows two repeats in warp and filling.

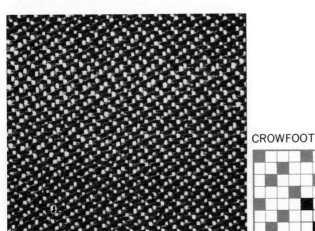

CROWFOOT

5. Crowfoot satin weave, an irregular filling-faced weave. Weave draft shows two repeats in warp and filling.

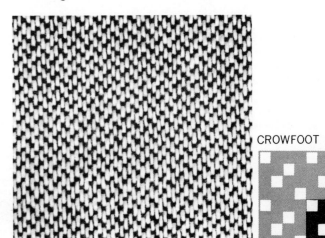

CROWFOOT

6. Crowfoot satin weave, an irregular warp-faced weave. Weave draft shows two repeats in warp and filling.

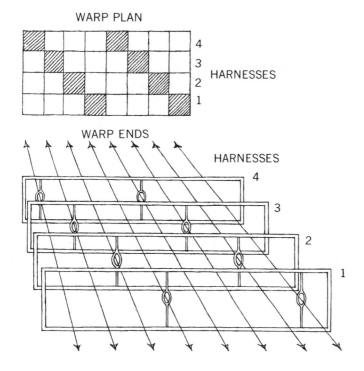

WARP PLAN

WARP ENDS

HARNESSES

4

3

2

1

THREADING ACCORDING TO WARP PLAN

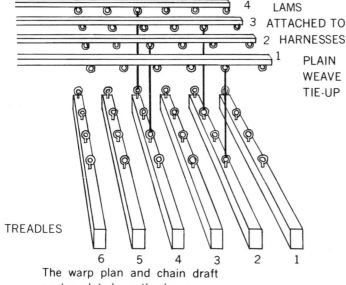

4 LAMS
3 ATTACHED TO
2 HARNESSES
1

PLAIN
WEAVE
TIE-UP

TREADLES

6 5 4 3 2 1

The warp plan and chain draft
as translated on the loom.

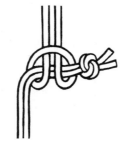

Knot used for connecting
lams to treadles.

In order to see our weave realized the way we had created it, we must be sure the warp is threaded through the heddles correctly. This brings us to the warp plan. As before, every vertical space in the graph paper is a warp end, *but,* now every horizontal space is a harness. The harnesses on the loom are numbered from front to back. On paper, from the bottom up, unless otherwise indicated.

Straight Draw

The warp plan that will give us any of the weaves already illustrated is the *straight draw.* Two repeats of a 4-harness straight draw are shown as drafted on graph paper, left, and as threaded through the heddles. The repeats are in the width of the warp since there is as yet no filling.

To translate the straight draw, start with the lower right-hand corner. The first square on harness #1 is filled in. This means the first end on the right goes through a heddle on the first harness. Continuing to the left we find an empty square on harness #1 but a filled-in one directly above on harness #2. This means the second warp end goes through a heddle on the second harness. The third warp end then goes through a heddle on the third harness and the fourth end on the fourth harness. The fifth end is on harness #1 and begins the second repeat. The unit of repeat in a 4-harness straight draw is four ends, which means that every fourth end will be woven alike.

No warp end goes through more than one heddle and the filled-in square in the draft means one warp end threaded through one heddle on one harness.

Treadles are tied to lams according to the chain draft. Lams are levers that lie between treadles and harnesses and are numbered according to the harnesses they are tied to. Pressing on the treadles pulls on the lams which in turn raises or lowers the harnesses. The treadles have been numbered from right to left.

Treadle #2 is tied to harnesses #1 and #3. Treadle #4 is tied to harnesses #2 and #4. This tie-up is for plain weave.

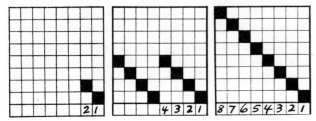

Straight draw shown on two, four, and eight harnesses. Numbers below drafts refer to harnesses.

This is the most common warp plan and can be done on any number of harnesses, from 2 to 16. The warp ends are pulled through consecutive harness heddles and, on graph paper, the threading forms a diagonal line.

Irregular Threading

On a 2-harness loom this draw produces only a plain weave. In order to achieve different weave effects, you would have to design an irregular threading pattern, such as the one below. Using this threading, the weave repeats on 12 ends and, if there is a pick used in each shed, on 2 picks, and looks exactly like the drawing-in draft.

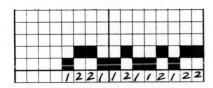

A 2-harness warp plan in an irregular threading pattern.

Even Point Draw

Another fairly common warp plan is the *point*. The unit of repeat, if used on a 4-harness loom, is 6 ends. The fifth end is no longer on harness #1, as in the straight draw, but on #3. The sixth end is on harness #2. This draw used with the even-balanced or the reverse twill produces the patterns at right, below. These are known as "rose path" variations.

By studying the warp plan and weave draft below right, you can see that wherever the same harness occurs, the weave over it remains the same. For example, follow the weave up the paper wherever it falls on harness #2. You will see it is always two filled-in squares, followed by three empty squares, then three filled-in squares, then three empty ones, ending with one filled-in square. This is so because every time a harness is raised, all warp ends threaded through that harness must also raise. All ends threaded through harness #2 heddles will raise and weave the same throughout the width of the warp. All ends on harness #1 will weave whenever that harness is raised, all those on harness #3 will weave whenever that one is raised, and all those on harness #4 will weave when that harness is raised.

The harness numbers are at the bottom of the warp plan. Please keep in mind that the weaves show 2 repeats in the warp and filling.

"ROSE PATH"—TWO VARIATIONS

The $\frac{2}{2}$ twill weave (right) drafted over the even point draw. The numbers on the side indicate the chain draft. The $\frac{2}{2}$ reverse twill weave (far right) over the even point draw. Two repeats are shown in filling and warp.

A 4-harness even point warp plan, showing two repeats.

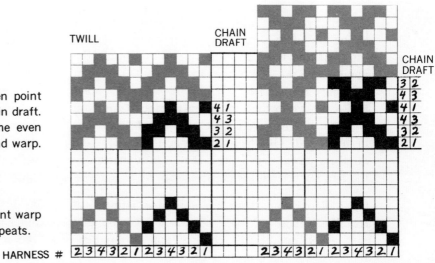

HARNESS #

CHAIN DRAFT

All that is lacking now is a plan to tell you which harnesses to raise and in what order. This plan is called the chain draft. We can figure out the chain draft from one repeat of the weave. The vertical spaces indicate a harness and the horizontal spaces the filling. On a 4-harness loom our chain draft will never be any wider than four spaces.

For the plain weave, the chain reads as below:

On a floor loom, the tie-ups of the treadles are:

2-harness loom—First shed, treadle #1 tied to harness #1.
　　　　　　　Second shed, treadle #2 tied to harness #2.
4-harness loom—First shed, treadle #1 tied to harnesses #1 and #3.
　　　　　　　Second shed, treadle #2 tied to harnesses #2 and #4.

On a table loom, the following levers must be pressed:

2-harness loom—First shed, lever raising harness #1.
　　　　　　　Second shed, lever raising harness #2.
4-harness loom—First shed, levers raising harnesses #1 and #3.
　　　　　　　Second shed, levers raising harnesses #2 and #4.

In the following two patterns, I have used x's for the warp plan and chain draft, so that it can be seen at a glance that these two drafts are not part of the weave draft.

PATTERN #1

Commonly called "goose-eye," this pattern belongs to the twill family of weaves. There are 2 repeats shown in the warp and 1 in the filling. Study the numbers on the side of the chain draft. On the first pick only one harness is raised in order to obtain the weave. Follow the chain draft upwards, and you will see that for every pick only one harness has to be raised. On the table loom just follow the numbers upwards and press the lever connected to the harness desired for that pick.

On a floor loom there are a limited number of treadles, usually six for a 4-harness loom. Be sure that every number, or combination of numbers, found in the chain draft is connected to a treadle.

This is known as the tie-up. In pattern #1, there are four different numbers, each attached to a separate treadle and pressed according to the way it falls in the chain draft. Study the numbers on the chain draft and on the warp plan more closely. You will see that they read upwards in the same sequence as they do from right to left. When this occurs in a draft, it is to be "woven, or treadled, as drawn-in." In this instance the chain draft is not necessary since the pattern can be achieved by simply following the harness order from right to left.

Please note that should you decide to change your chain draft and press the first eight numbers and then repeat them, you will no longer have the goose-eye, but a type of herringbone weave.

PATTERN #2

"M's and O's," is an attractive texture weave. For this pattern two harnesses are attached on every treadle. In all, there are four different number combinations. Attach four treadles to the four combinations. The middle row of numbers is the actual treadle number that is pressed. The row of numbers on the far right is a further shortening of the instructions and indicates that each combination of treadles must be pressed twice.

Some weavers prefer to have each treadle attached to a different harness and then use both feet to press two treadles. In this case, the treadles are used exactly as the levers on the table loom.

NOTE: The drafts I show throughout are designed for the rising shed loom. For a loom with a sinking shed, reverse the draft indications so that the empty squares for the rising shed loom become the filled-in squares for the sinking shed loom, and vice versa. After the weave draft is adjusted, plot the chain draft accordingly. Be careful of the filling-faced and warp-faced weaves because they are virtually impossible to attain on the sinking shed loom.

As I mentioned earlier, methods of writing drafts differ from school to school, from teacher to teacher, and from locale to locale. If you don't find drafts exactly as they are given in this book, don't be dismayed. As long as a draft contains the following information it will not be difficult to translate:

member that a filled-in square indicates a harness must be raised.

1. The number of harnesses the weave needs in order to be reproduced.
2. How to thread the loom for the desired weave.
3. What harnesses to raise and in what order. Re-

With these points in mind, you will soon become quite adept at translating drafts and will join in the weaver's common treasure hunt—that of finding new drafts and adapting them to your needs and loom.

PATTERN #1 **"Goose-Eye,"** a filling-faced weave based on a $\frac{1}{3}$ twill.

CHAIN DRAFT

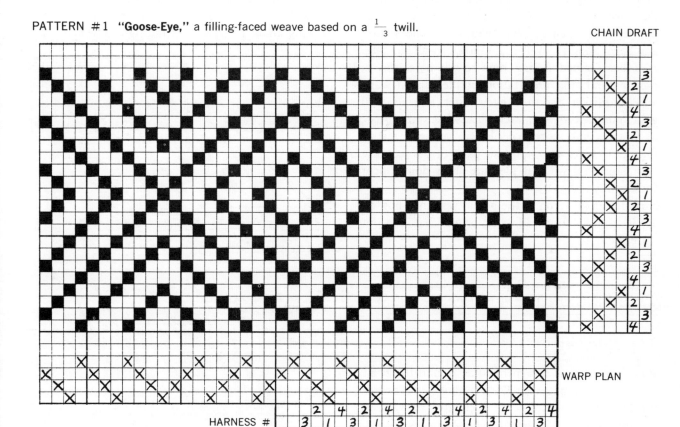

WARP PLAN

HARNESS #

PATTERN # 2
"M's and O's," showing a complete chain draft, and on the far right, its abbreviated version.

CHAIN
DRAFT TREADLES

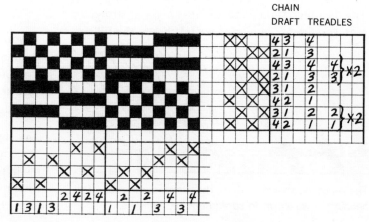

WARP PLAN

HARNESS #

STARTING TO WEAVE

The time has finally come when you are seated in front of the loom ready to weave. No matter how long or extensive your weaving career becomes, there will always be this thrill the moment you sit at the loom, open the first shed, throw the shuttle and begin another lovely rug, fabric, or wall hanging. If it has seemed a long time to get here, this is only natural; the preparation of the second warp will go quicker, the third even faster, and you will gain more speed with each successive warp. Also, as you become more experienced, you will realize that these tasks are important parts of the weaving craft, and you will get pleasure from doing them successfully.

Now, let us move on to the actual weaving—how to do it, pitfalls to avoid, and errors that can be corrected.

WEAVING ON THE 4-HARNESS LOOM

The Heading

When the warp is tied in bundles around the front apron bar (see pages 36-37, Beaming and Threading the Loom), spaces occur at certain intervals. By weaving a 1″ to 2″ heading, these spaces will be closed and the warp will lie in a straight line from the reed to the point of weaving. The smaller the individual bundle, the narrower the heading used. The heading should be of heavy yarn, string, or rags, (preferably in a color contrasting to the filling),

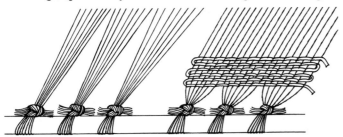

The warp is shown tied to the front apron bar. The heading is woven in to spread out the bundles.

in order to spread the bundles quickly and not to waste the warp. The heading yarn is wound in butterflies or on a stick shuttle and beaten down quite heavily.

Open Shed #1

Press the treadle, or lever, and open shed #1. Pass the shuttle through from right to left, allowing the filling thread to remain behind in the shed, and extending about 2″ outside of the right selvedge.

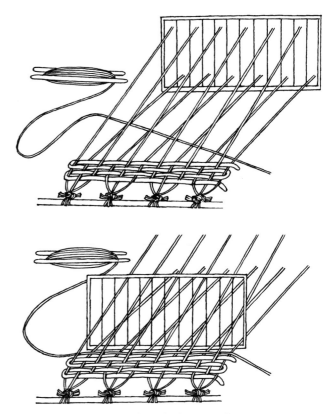

Beginning to weave after the heading has been put in.

If you are using the boat shuddle, hold it in your right hand between thumb and middle fingers. A sharp forward thrust of the index finger should provide the force needed to land the shuttle on the left edge of the weaving.

The shuttle glides on the taut warp ends that form the underside of the shed. The filling thread should be left in the shed at an angle—the lowest point where the thread enters and the highest where it exits. If it is left lying in a straight line, a taut,

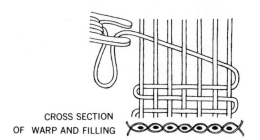

CROSS SECTION
OF WARP AND FILLING

The filling is placed in the shed on a diagonal so that the yarn has enough slack to interlace with the warp ends, avoiding a pulled-in line.

pulled-in line will result since there would not be enough "give" in the yarn to interlace with the warp.

Using the Beater

Grasp the top of the beater firmly in the center so that the pressure of the beat is spread evenly along the filling as it is pushed down into the warp. If you handle the beater more to one side than the other, you will find your web growing larger at a slant. Pull the beater forward with a swift, sharp movement.

Change to Shed #2

Return the beater to its original position and change to shed #2. Beat down once more. The force of the beat depends on the temperament of the weaver, the type of fabric being woven, and the feeling for the beat that a weaver develops. Some weavers have a heavy beat, and it is difficult for them to adapt themselves to doing very loose fabrics. Of others, the reverse is true, and they tap lightly instead of beating firmly. You will find that your beat can change with your mood. On a day when you are mad at the world, the beat tends to be firm and aggressive. On days of peace and quiet, the touch is apt to be lighter. Ideally, the beat should be a firm, but controlled, movement so that the picks per inch will be even throughout the entire woven piece.

Consider the Selvedge

After the second beat, pass the shuttle from left to right, leaving the filling thread snugly around

An even selvedge (left) with the filling turned correctly around the selvedge ends. An uneven selvedge (right), caused by turning the filling too loosely or too tightly.

the left selvedge. Maintain an even selvedge—the filling should not hang out beyond in a loop nor should it pull in tightly. There will be a normal amount of draw-in from selvedge to selvedge, but anything beyond this should be avoided since some of these pulled-in selvedge ends could be cut by the beater.

Inspect Warp and Make Necessary Adjustments

Continue weaving in this manner until the bundles are properly spaced. During this time any mistakes in drawing-in or sleying should be corrected and uneven tension remedied.

Warp End Threaded Incorrectly If the mistake is in the drawing-in, the warp end must be removed

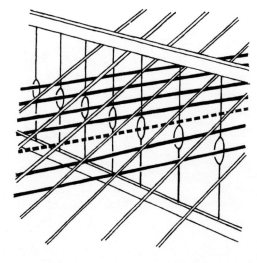

The dotted line indicates a warp end being drawn through a heddle left empty because of incorrect threading.

from the bundle and redrawn correctly. If the harness does not have an empty heddle to accommodate the misplaced warp end, tie a makeshift string heddle onto the harness bars.

Missing Warp End If there is a missing warp end, this can be corrected by making a string heddle on the necessary harness and inserting a warp end of the length needed. One side of this new warp end is tied in the bundle and the other around a spool that is allowed to hang from the back of the loom. Weight the spool so that the new end will have the same tension as the rest of the warp. Resley the ends in the reed to accommodate this new end.

Extra Warp End If there is an extra warp end, remove it and resley the reed correctly. If this leaves the heddle without a warp end running through it, it will not interfere with either the weaving or the spacing of the warp.

Incorrect Sleying Warp ends are sometimes twisted behind the reed by incorrect sleying. Remove the guilty ends from the bundle and pull them out of the reed. Untwist and resley correctly. If there is a skipped dent or too many ends per dent, resley that section of the warp so affected.

As all this illustrates, it is better to take the time to check back every 2″ or 3″ while drawing-in and sleying instead of having to take even more time to correct these errors later.

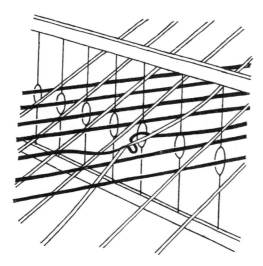

The above shows how warp ends can become twisted when incorrectly sleyed.

Uneven Tension A wavy line in the filling means uneven tension. The bundles must be retied at the points where the tension is not correct.

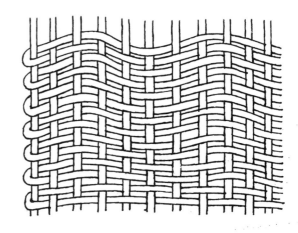

Wavy lines in the filling caused by uneven tension in the warp. The tension must be corrected.

Finish Off Heading

As soon as spaces are closed and mistakes corrected, cut the heading thread from the shuttle so that it extends about 1″ beyond the selvedge. This heading will prevent unraveling when the project is finished and taken off the loom. Also a few picks of the heading can be put in at the end of the project until you decide how you want to finish it off, whether by knots, fringes, hemming, or stitching by either hand or machine. If you are doing plain weave, you should end the heading on the second shed.

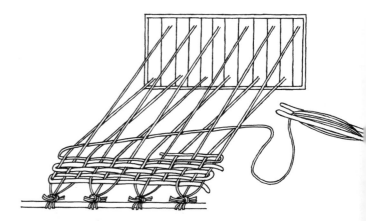

Tuck in the new filling yarn that extends beyond the right selvedge and bring it to the back of the weaving.

The Filling

Take your shuttle with the filling yarn and begin exactly as you did for the heading, except when you open the second shed, insert the yarn that had been left to extend beyond the right selvedge. In the heading it was not important to tuck in the beginning and end of the yarn, but in the project itself, the ends must be brought back into the warp and out the back side.

Piecing the Yarn

When you start a new bobbin of the same thread, you can "piece" the yarn by laying the new thread beside the old one. Make sure they overlap for about 1½", then beat into position.

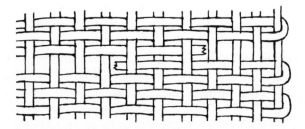

Piecing the filling threads by laying the new thread over the old one in the same shed.

Weaving with Two Colors

If you are weaving with two different colors and the color repeat is small, it is not necessary to cut

When weaving with two colors, the color not in use is carried along the selvedge until used again. This is a method for narrow color repeats. Note the start of the filling thread tucked back into shed.

the thread with every color change. When you finish with color #1, lay the shuttle aside, allowing the thread to hang loosely from the fabric. Pick up color #2 shuttle and continue to weave. Every time you are on the same side as color #1, go under it with the #2 shuttle and bring it alongside the selvedge as illustrated below left.

Bringing the Warp Forward

Continue weaving as long as the shed opening is wide enough to accommodate the shuttle and the beater has enough space in which to beat down. When this is no longer possible, slowly release the back ratchet so that a small supply of warp can be brought to the weaving position. Roll the fabric around the cloth beam until the last pick woven is as far as it can be from the reed and yet still can be reached by the beater. If necessary, release a bit more warp from the warp beam. Then secure the ratchets, adjust the tension until it is taut enough, and continue weaving.

If you have released too much warp, rewind the excess back onto the warp beam.

Broken Warp End

To replace a broken warp end, measure out a new end the length of the warp yet to be woven, plus 4" to 6". Tie it in a bowknot to the broken end at the back of the loom. Remove the broken end from the dent and heddle, thread the new end through in its place allowing it to overlap the web by about 4". Secure the front of the new end around a straight pin inserted into the web about 1" or 2" forward from the last pick. Untie bowknot and pull the new end until it has the same tension as the rest of the warp, then retie.

As the weaving progresses, and the warp moves forward, the bowknot will come closer to the back harness. You must watch for this and untie it when it gets too close. Then retie it at the whiproll.

When the project is finished, pull all broken ends and new ends through to the back of the weaving with a darning needle and trim.

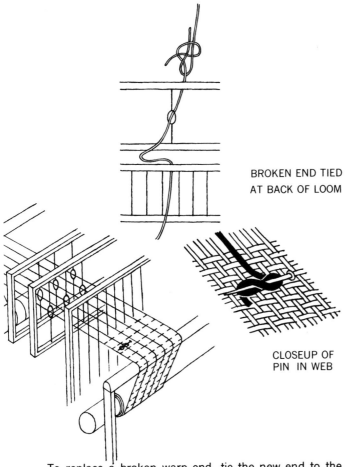

BROKEN END TIED
AT BACK OF LOOM

CLOSEUP OF
PIN IN WEB

To replace a broken warp end, tie the new end to the broken end at the back of the loom. It is then secured at the front of the loom around a pin inserted into the web.

Measuring the Weave

Have a tape measure handy to keep track of how much you have woven and to make sure your picks per inch are constant. Insert a pin or loop a piece of yarn around the selvedge every time you have measured the length.

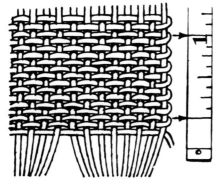

Measuring the number of picks per inch with a tape measure.

To Remove the Weaving

At the end of your weaving, cut the project off and untie or cut it from the front apron bar, allowing enough unwoven warp ends to remain for the finishing. As mentioned earlier, heavy filling can be woven in for about 1″ at the end of the project.

To Tie a New Warp

If you plan to use the same warp plan and sleying arrangement on your next warp, then cut the warp in front of the beater. Tie it in slipknots so it will not be pulled out of the reed and heddles. The new warp can then be tied onto the remaining warp.

To tie a new warp to an old one, place the warp chain, with lease sticks in the cross, in front of the beater. Secure the lease sticks in position and cut the loop end of the new warp. Tie the ends in consecutive order to the old warp. When all the ends have been tied, work the knots slowly through the reed, then through the heddles. Be sure to roll back the slack that will exist between the beater and harnesses. Continue beaming as explained on pages 36-37.

NOTE: The important processes of weaving can be broken down into four basic steps.

1. Open the shed.
2. Beat the previous filling.
3. Pass the shuttle through shed carrying the new filling pick.
4. Beat new pick into position.

The goals to strive for in weaving are an even beat and even selvedges.

WEAVING ON THE FRAME LOOM

Weaving on the frame loom is a very simple process but not a fast one since making the two sheds requires more handwork than on a table or floor loom. However, because the hands are so involved with the warp, a comfortable intimacy and rapport develop between the weaver and his work.

Making the First Shed

Make the chain spacer. (See page 39.) Open the first shed with the shed stick and insert filling. The filling can be carried on a small stick shuttle (good to use when one color is carried from selvedge to selvedge), flute, bobbin, or butterfly. (See pages 40-41.) Do not pull the filling through tightly but leave it in the shed at a diagonal. Close shed.

Beat down filling with short sharp taps starting from the side you entered. A tapestry comb or table fork can be used for this.

SHED #1

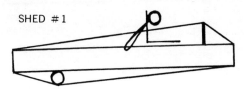

Making the Second Shed—Method #1

There are two ways to open the second shed. One is to pull the string heddles down and out towards yourself, thereby lifting the even-numbered warp ends. However, since it is possible to grasp only a limited amount of heddles in your hand, you must work your way across the warp in sections. I usually proceed from right to left. Left hand pulls on heddles as right hand inserts filling, pushing it from one open section to the other until left selvedge is reached. Beat down as for first shed.

SHED #2

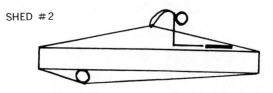

Making the Second Shed—Method #2

This is probably the easiest method when you want one filling color across the entire warp. Unscrew and lift heddle rod. It in turn lifts all the even-numbered warp ends. Have a second shed stick at hand and insert it into the opening. If the opening is too small to allow this, push your original shed stick to the top of the loom as far as it will go. Insert the second stick and release heddle rod. Open shed, and insert filling. Remove stick and beat down. The stick can be used to push down the filling,

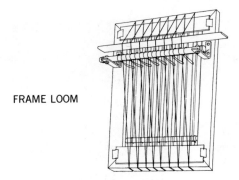

FRAME LOOM

but the comb must be used to beat down firmly. Check that all even-numbered ends have been lifted.

Moving the Warp Down

When you have woven as close as possible to the heddle rod and no longer have a wide comfortable shed, remove one of the front tension sticks. Then push up on the warp-end bar and revolve the woven warp slowly around the bottom of the frame. Stop when the last pick woven is about 2″ from the top of the bottom frame.

Keeping Selvedges Even

At times it will be difficult to keep selvedges even and the woven piece from narrowing. To remedy both problems thread a tapestry needle with warp thread and run the thread through the selvedges every 2″ or 3″. Tie the thread around the frame sides, making sure it is taut enough to keep the weaving spread to its intended width. As the warp revolves, these threads are pushed down the sides or cut.

At Completion

When the project is completed, cut the warp off at the warp-end bar, remove the chain spacer, and finish off the piece as you had planned.

NOTE: The process of weaving on the frame loom is broken down into four steps:

1. Open shed #1 (odd-numbered ends) with shed stick, insert filling.
2. Close shed and beat down filling.
3. Open shed #2 (even-numbered ends) by working heddle strings, insert filling.
4. Close shed and beat down filling.

Table mat woven of strips of velvet, satin, and yarn in plain weave with the soumak stitch. When sides are joined, this becomes an accessory bag.

ACCESSORY BAG OR TABLE MAT

Plain Weave with Soumak Stitch

I am sure that in your home you have many pieces of fabric—clothing, drapery, towels, or remnants left over from sewing—that you are about to throw out. Don't, for these fabrics, cut into strips, can provide us with the filling for our first project—an accessory bag. This bag will carry the yarn, bobbins, scissors, and other tools that you will accumulate in your weaving life. It can be used also as a shopping bag or, if the selvedges are very straight, you can piece two or three lengths together to make a small scatter rug.

In this project, we will be concerned mostly with the first basic weave, the plain weave (see pages 42-43), and a novelty technique called "soumak." Soumak is a finger-manipulated weave, which means that even on a table or floor loom it must be put in by hand and not by the raising or lowering of harnesses. It is an Oriental carpet tapestry weave and produces a raised diagonal effect which is a way to achieve surface interest in a two-shed loom.

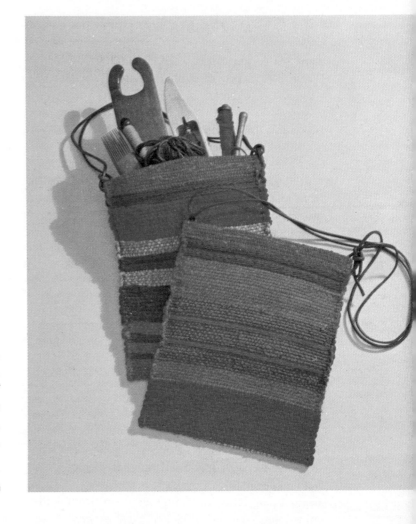

Accessory bag with leather thong handles. It is a useful carry-all for holding weaving utensils. Instructions on following page.

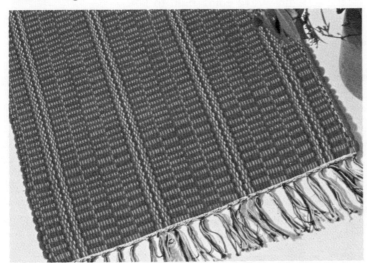

Felt strips instead of rags were used by H. G. Kargus to make this attractive rug.

Unique carry-all bag, using twine, jute and string, made by Ahza Cohen.

MATERIALS NEEDED

Warp 8/4 cotton carpet warp, about 160 yds.

Filling 1 to 2 lbs. of cloth cut into 1" wide strips and pieced together, as shown, so that you have a continuous strip with which to weave. The cloth may be of any fiber content, but I generally try to keep all shrinkables together in one project and non-shrinkables in another. In the bag illustrated here, I used taffeta from an old evening gown, velvet from an old blouse, and corduroy and cotton from my sewing scrap basket. Also have lengths of heavy yarn to use in the soumak sections.

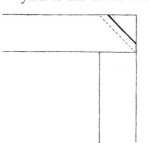

Piece the rags at right angles prior to winding them on shuttles. The seam is trimmed to eliminate bulk in the material.

CALCULATIONS

Sett 10 ends per inch. Double last two ends on each side for selvedge. Total number of ends, 104.

Width on Loom 10"

Length *frame loom,* a continuous warp around the entire loom (see pages 38-39); *table or floor loom,* dressed length is 1½ yds.

Finished Length 24"

WARP PLAN

For a floor or table loom, thread on a straight draw (page 46) and follow the directions on page 48 for the making of two sheds. Directions for the frame are on page 55.

TECHNIQUES

Soumak Stitch

Plain weave is used throughout except in areas indicated as soumak. Soumak is made as follows:

1. Weave a row of plain weave, from right to left.

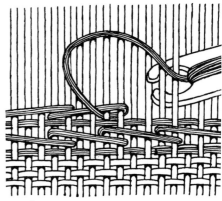

A right to left slant of soumak stitch is shown in 2nd row of dark filling. Reverse slant is seen in unfinished row.

This is the beginning of the yarn section so you should have the beginning of this pick extending beyond the selvedge at the right. Tuck in the extended yarn on the right in the same shed.

2. Have the warp in a neutral position (a closed shed). Count in 6 ends from the left and insert shuttle front to back between the 6th and 7th ends.

3. Bring shuttle back to surface by inserting it, back to front, 2 ends to the left between the 4th and 5th ends, *over* the surface filling.

4. Count over 6 ends from this new position and repeat as in #3 and #4.

5. Continue in this manner across the width of the warp.

6. Beat the filling into place and weave a pick of plain weave going right to left.

7. Begin a second row of soumak as above, *except* this time when you go under the 2 ends bring the shuttle to the surface *under* the filling yarn already on the surface. This will change the slant of the stitch.

Soumak can have many variations. It can be brought over 2, 3, 4, or 5 ends instead of 6. This depends on the sett, since too long a float is not desirable. There can be many rows of plain weave in between the soumak rows, but at least one row is needed to bind down the soumak. The soumak does not have to extend across the entire row, but can be used instead as a random effect or to achieve a motif. If you pull tightly on the 2 enclosed ends, gaps may occur in the warp. For the purpose of this project, it is advisable not to pull this tightly and to concentrate instead on keeping the threads aligned.

DESIGN

I have used a random stripe pattern determined by the amount of strips I had in each of the various fabrics. Since the fiber content of the fabrics was almost all different, I strove for unity through color, choosing only those fabrics that looked well together. If you have an odd assortment that seems to have no color unity, try dyeing them all with the same color. The colors will still be different, but they should have a common glow. Naturally, the effectiveness of this depends on the fiber content of your cloth. For information on how to dye, turn to page 24.

Pick your fabrics with a thought for textural contrasts and remember you can use scraps of yarn for the soumak or for the fine stripes.

HELPFUL HINTS

1. After you have cut and stitched the strips, wind each color around a stick shuttle, attaching the strip by a slip knot around the arm of the shuttle. Do not try to handle lengths of more than 10 yds. at a time or the shuttle will become bulky and unwieldy.

2. Use a firm beat but do not expect the warp to be covered completely. Plan, therefore, on having the warp color show and choose its color in accordance with the filling you have on hand.

3. A heading, woven of yarn, can be made at the beginning and end of the project. It should be about 1½″ wide and not beaten in very firmly since it should be pliable enough to be folded back as the hem. Fringe the project if a hem is not used. You should allow at least 4″ of warp for the fringing but trim to about 2″ after the fringe is made.

4. Be sure that the joining seams in the strips are folded toward the inside so they do not show. Also,

PATTERN FOR ACCESSORY BAG

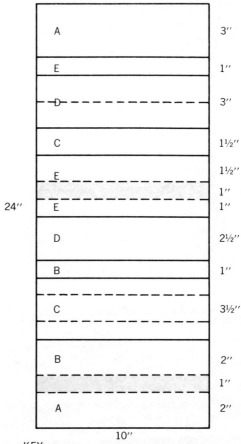

KEY:
Dotted lines—one row of Soumak stitch
Gray areas —solid Soumak
Numbers —width of stripes
Letters —arrangement of colors

all fabrics that have a right and wrong side, like napped fabrics, should be folded and beaten in to show the right side to advantage. When starting a new color, taper the ends of both rag strips to be joined so that the overlapping will not be thick and create a hump.

FINISHING

1. Trim the back side of the project.

2. Put wrong sides of bag together and sew seams.

3. Braid a handle for your bag using heavy yarn or attach leather thong strips in any length you want.

RYA RUG

Plain Weave with Rug Knots

One of the most luxuriant and decorative pieces you can have in your home is a rya rug. The rya rug has a thick pile about 1½″ to 2″ high that adds depth to the colors used.

These rugs come to us from Scandinavia where in olden days their deep pile was necessary for warmth on board ships during winter sealing and fishing trips and as "throws" in sleighs. They were used as coverings on beds and were hung on walls and placed on floors for added protection against the cold.

As they became less of a practical necessity, their patterns became more ornamental and colorful. Today the designing and making of rya rugs is considered an art form.

The rug consists of warp, filling, and the Ghiordes knot. This knot has been used in Oriental carpeting since the 14th century. It is wound around two warp ends. Oriental rugs, which have a very short pile, have between 80 to 320 knots per square inch and a minimum of filling shots to hold the pile in place. Our rya adaptation will have only 8 to 10 knots per square inch and, because of the height of the pile, about ¾″ of filling between each row of knots.

Our rug will be made in 10″ squares, woven separately, then sewn together. Narrow looms or frame looms can accommodate this size easily. But the size is quite flexible; if you make approximately a 6′ x 4′ now and decide to change the size later, you do so by simply removing squares or weaving additional ones.

If you should want to make one or two experimental squares, they can always be used as ornamental pieces of color on the wall or on footstools or as pillow covers. The underside of the pillow can be canvas or plain weave.

(Opposite) "Chartres," a hand-knotted rya rug 5′ by 6′, with a 2″ pile. The design was inspired by the stained glass windows of that cathedral.

MATERIALS NEEDED

Overall Size of Rug This is a matter of personal preference. A good area rug size is 6′ x 4′. The nearest size to this, using our 10″ square, would be 70″ x 50″.

Warp 8/4 cotton carpet warp. A rug 7 squares by 5 squares, or 70″ by 50″, requires about 3900 yds. One 10″ square made on a 20″ by 16″ frame loom requires about 110 yds. If you are doing this on a floor or table loom, you can make a longer warp and do several samples on one warp. At least 4 squares could be woven on a 3-yd. warp; in that case, you will need 280 yds. for each warp. The color of the warp is not important since it will be completely covered by the filling. Linen warp yarn can be used, but it is somewhat more expensive.

Filling 3- or 4-ply wool rug yarn or heavy cotton rug filler. About 5 lbs., in a color to go with the pile, are needed for a rug 7 squares by 5 squares. A soft twist yarn covers the warp more easily than a hard twist. Weaving the ground goes quicker with a heavy yarn, but, in some cases of very heavy yarn, parts of the warp will remain exposed. I prefer to cover the warp completely, but since this is the underside of the rug, it is really your choice as to whether or not you want the warp exposed.

Pile Plan to use a total of about 10 lbs. of rug wool. In the two designs illustrated here, there are predominantly two colors equally divided, requiring about 5 lbs. each. However, you will notice I did

A 10″ square of the rya rug made on the frame loom showing back and front. Notice the Swedish braid (see page 65) on two sides of square at left.

not use just one color in an area, but three or four shades of one color in the 3- or 4-ply yarn. This gives a color subtlety and interest that cannot be achieved with a single yarn of heavy rug weight.

Should you wish to have different shades of a color, divide your poundage equally between them. I heartily recommend making one experimental square in your chosen color scheme before ordering the complete amounts. You can use yarns that you have at home, even though they may have no color unity. Try giving them a related hue by over-dyeing as mentioned on page 24.

There are "rug yarns" specifically marked as such. These are generally what I use although I am a great believer in mixing rug yarns with others of different weight, fiber content, and texture. A bit of linen gives an added lustrous quality to a rug. A hard twist yarn, together with a soft twist, provides textural interest, as does a strand or two of fine yarn mixed with a heavier one.

CALCULATIONS

Sett 8 ends per inch. Double last 2 ends on each side for selvedge. Total number of ends, 92.
Width on Loom 11″.
Length *frame loom,* a continuous warp; *table or floor loom,* 16″ for each square. Allow 10″ for the square and about 3″ at each end so that the cut warp can be braided back.

WARP PLAN

Thread on a straight draw, refer to page 47, for a table or floor loom. Use plain weave as the ground weave.

DESIGN

There are two design possibilities offered here for the rya rug. However, if you have an idea of your own that you want to try, the following instructions will help you prepare your design.

To Prepare Design

1. A color sketch is not necessary if your design is simple, but I would advise having one if it is complex. The color sketch should be in scale to the dimensions of your rug, but does not have to be full size.

2. Draw your design in outline and in full size. Use heavy wrapping paper or paper bags taped together.

3. Divide the pattern and color sketch into 10″ squares. Use these to check against the pattern during weaving.

4. Consider where you plan to use the rug and place the outline sketch there together with yarn or fabrics in the colors you plan to order. In this way you can study the effects of the yarns and colors in your room before any purchasing is done and you have to return excess material.

PATTERNS

To develop Pattern 1, draw a 10″ square with a diagonal line running across it. Place this behind your weaving to be sure the design changes from a dark to light color at the correct knots.

Pattern 2 is also drawn on a 10″ square. Find the center of the square and draw a 7″ circle. (A child's compass can be used or a plate near to this size.) Put diagram behind weaving to be sure the color changes come at the correct knots. The circle in your weaving will never be an exact circle but an impression of one, because of the length of the knots. It will, however, be a more interesting pattern.

NOTE: If you have the facilities, both of these patterns can be woven in a larger square size than 10″.

Color

Your choice of colors depends on where you intend to use the rug. If the combinations shown here fit your color schemes, use them. If not, let them be a guide to the colors you need.

Pattern 1 has a very dramatic contrast of colors. To follow this guide, choose a dark color for the brown area and a light one for the gold area. If you like the pattern, but the contrast is too extreme for your room setting, choose either a lighter color for the brown area or a darker color for the gold area. But be careful not to get the two colors so close in value that you cannot see the difference between them. The coloring of this pattern is based on a difference in value.

Pattern 2 has its coloring based on a difference in hue. Choose colors of close values but not of the same color family. The result is a much more subtle effect than Pattern 1. Should you want to make this more striking, try colors of vastly different values.

In Pattern 1, I worked from a deep value to a light value of one color family. To make this gradation, I changed one strand in each knot to a lighter value as I knotted across the warp. For example, if one knot was made up of three strands of deep gold, the knot next to it would have two strands of deep gold and one of a lighter gold. Then the next knot would have only one strand of deep gold and two of lighter gold. It is not necessary, however, to change value with every knot.

Pattern 2 has three close shades of each color. Unlike Pattern 1, they are not graded from dark to light but are combined in every other knot.

TECHNIQUES

Background Plain weave is used for the background of the rug; it should be an old friend from Project #1. Now, however, it is made with yarn and completely covers the warp. Beat well, to hold the knots securely in place.

Preparing the Pile The rya knot can be made in one of two ways:

Method #1 Cut the yarn beforehand into 4″ long pieces. To precut it, make a 4″ wide gauge of heavy cardboard or wood and wind the yarn around the gauge. Slit the yarn at each edge of the gauge with a razor blade or sharp knife. This is a good method

These diagrams suggest pattern possibilities for two simple geometric designs.

PATTERN #1—DIAGONAL MOTIF (Seen on page 64)

10″ / 10″

The diagonal motif can be arranged to form many patterns. The border pattern at right has diagonal squares at top and bottom only; the rest are solid. Thirty-five squares are needed, seven in length and 5 in width.

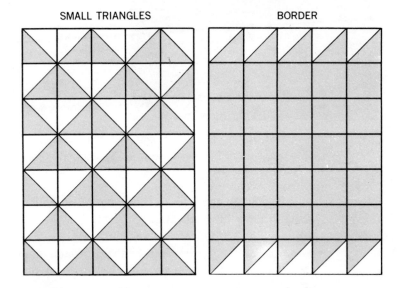

SMALL TRIANGLES · BORDER

The circle motif can be used in an alternated pattern, or centered. Thirty-five squares are needed.

PATTERN #2—CIRCULAR MOTIF (Seen on page 61)

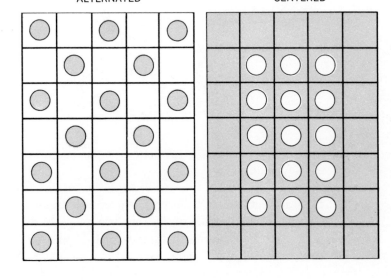

ALTERNATED · CENTERED

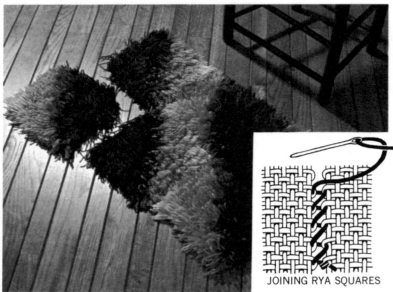

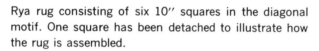

JOINING RYA SQUARES

Rya rug consisting of six 10″ squares in the diagonal motif. One square has been detached to illustrate how the rug is assembled.

The same rug squares rearranged to form a different pattern. Innumerable designs are possible with the simple diagonal pattern.

to use if you change colors in the knots frequently. I usually have the yarn arranged around me with each color in a small box, then I just pick up the colors I need for a knot and tie them around the warp. The strands of the yarn do not have to be the exact same size, but there should be no difference greater than an inch.

Method #2 Make butterflies of the yarn and colors you plan to use together. As the butterfly goes around

PILE GAUGES

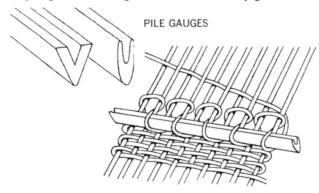

Wind yarn around gauge; cut along groove in gauge to form pile.

the warp ends to form the knot, it goes also around a gauge on the surface of the rug. The gauge is 2″ high and can be made of cardboard. It should be the length of your square. More elaborate gauges

can be made of metal or wood, with a slit on top so that a razor can glide over and cut the knot loops. With the cardboard gauge, the loops can be cut with scissors.

Ghiordes Knot The knot is made over two warp ends. Working from left to right, the yarn goes down between two ends, then under the left end, up and over the left and right ends, under the right end, and up between the two ends. The two yarn ends meet in the center and are pulled tightly forward and up.

If you are using a butterfly, the gauge is laid over the yarn; the butterfly goes over it and to the next set of warp ends for the next knot. As you make

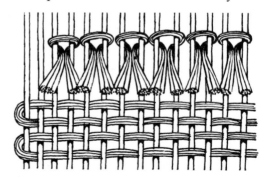

Ghiordes knot shown after being cut. The next pick of plain weave will push down the knots and secure them firmly in the woven web.

this knot, pull up tightly on the yarn, but not so tightly as to buckle the gauge. The gauge will stand on end when the yarn is tightened around it. Proceed to the end of your row or color, always remembering to go under and over the gauge between each set of knotted warp ends.

STEPS IN CONSTRUCTION

1. Weave 1″ of plain weave. Be sure you leave at least 2″ of warp before the first pick. This will later be turned under and braided over the 1″ of plain weave.

2. Tie a row of rya knots. The end selvedge threads, which are doubled, (one doubled end on each side), are left without knots. The knots are made with the warp in a neutral position. If you are using the gauge, cut the knot loops and remove gauge.

3. Take the shuttle with the filling yarn and go twice around the empty end selvedge threads. Weave a pick of plain weave. Do not use the same shed that you wove in before the row of knots.

4. Change sheds. Go twice around the empty end selvedge threads on the other side of the square. Weave a pick of plain weave.

5. Continue with plain weave for ¾″.

6. Tie the second row of knots.

7. Repeat steps 3, 4, and 5 and continue in this manner for 10 rows of knots.

8. After you have finished the 10th row of knots, weave ¼″ plain weave, making sure to beat extra hard to insure the knots against slipping out.

9. On the frame loom, measure up on the warp at least 2″ and cut off the sample. On a long warp, on the floor or table loom, weave a piece of soft cardboard 2″ wide in a shed of plain weave. In the alternate shed of plain weave, insert another 2″ cardboard. This will give the needed lengths for the braid. You can now go on to the next square.

HELPFUL HINTS

1. Leave the filling yarn loose and at a diagonal in the shed before beating down. Otherwise, the selvedges will tend to pull in more than is allowed for. Strive for neat straight selvedges.

2. Put in more filling picks in the ground weave than necessary. Successive rows tend to beat down

the earlier rows so that you may end up with less than ¾″ between each row of knots.

FINISHING

1. Trim the back side of the square.

2. Braid the warp ends over the back of the square, using a *Swedish braid*. As you braid, push the strands of the braid with your thumb towards the square so that they will lie tightly against the square. Start at the back on the left and work over by twos. Take two ends and go under two, over two and under two. Bring the original two to the surface and point toward the top of the square. Take the next two ends at the left and work them under the next two, over and under and to the surface and point upward. Do this with all the warp ends until you have four pairs left at the right. Braid these into a 4-strand braid about 1″ long. Start from the left and tie the pairs of warp ends together so that you are assured of a firm edge when you sew the squares together.

3. Sew the squares together using a tapestry needle threaded with the same yarn or color as the filling. The yarn should be about twice the length of one side of your square. Place the squares to be sewn according to your pattern. Attach the yarn securely to the lower right edge by looping it a couple of times around either the braid or the filling. Pull the needle through the loop on the lower left side. This loop is made by either the braid or filling, depending on which side of the square you are sewing. The needle is pulled up through the loop and across to the right side, where it is pushed down through the loop. Continue in this manner to the top of the squares. At the end of the seam, take two or three loops to finish off. The 1″ braids can be sewn down at the same time or tacked down later with finer thread. Trim the warp ends when the seam is finished. The stitches of this seam can be spaced at about ⅛″ to ¼″ apart depending on the weight of your sewing yarn. Pull tightly enough so that the edges being sewn lie smoothly next to each other, but be careful not to overlap. One thing to watch for is that one of the squares does not shift while you are stitching or it will not match to the other square at the end of the seam.

(Above) Front of gold bag with tassels and braided handles. An example of the "straight laid-in" technique. Here the turns are made on the face of the fabric to add textural effect to the design. (Opposite page) Back of gold bag. Here the turns are made on the wrong side of the fabric, resulting in a smooth surface. This is an adaptation of the traditional Greek bag.

GREEK BAG

Plain Weave with Laid-in Technique

The laid-in or brocading technique permits us to "paint" with an additional filling thread in order to create varied pattern and color effects on a plain weave background. A great favorite of weavers in Europe, Mexico, and Central America, this technique is responsible for the beautiful peasant work that often resembles embroidery.

Although this bag is used as a carry-all, it can be a decorative hanging or a pillow cover as well. The technique is well adapted as trim on blankets, scarves, and table linens.

One common laid-in method is the "straight laid-in," as in the gold bag. Here the pattern filling yarn is placed in the same sheds as the background plain weave. It weaves back and forth over only the area prescribed by the design, while the background filling travels from selvedge to selvedge.

For the laid-in method, the beginner should choose a simple or geometric design, such as is illustrated here. The design can be drawn, full-size, on plain paper and placed as a guide in back of the weaving; or on graph paper with each square equal to the number of warp and filling threads determined by technique and yarns used.

Back of gold bag.

The color of the pattern thread should be in contrast to the background color so it does not blend in and become lost. Since the filling is not beaten down to cover the warp, the color of the warp must be considered as part of the background color.

This technique can be woven with either the right side or the wrong side towards the weaver. I prefer weaving on the right side, but care must be taken at the point where the pattern thread turns so that turns are uniformly and neatly accomplished.

Another adaptation of the Greek bag. The braid forming the handle continues across bottom of bag.

MATERIALS NEEDED—GOLD BAG

Warp 8/4 cotton, or linen or wool in a comparable weight, prepared for warp use. Black was used for the gold bag to tone down the brilliancy of color. The warp can be in the same color family as the filling or a complement or accent color. Approximately 250 yds. are needed—about 6 oz.

Filling and Pattern All yarn used was lighter-weight Nordic flossa.

4 oz. dull olive	2 oz. lemon yellow
2 oz. gold	4 oz. dark gold
4 oz. orange	

CALCULATIONS

Sett 10 ends per inch. Double last two ends on each side for selvedge. Total number of ends, 124.
Width on Loom 12″.
Length *Frame loom,* a continuous warp; *Table or floor loom,* 1 yd. plus loom allowance.

NOTE: Each side of bag is approximately 12″ wide and 12″ long, with a 1″ allowance to turn back for hem at the top opening of bag. Back and front are woven as a continuous piece.

Warp Plan Straight draw (See page 47).
Tie Up For plain weave.

STEPS IN CONSTRUCTION AND TECHNIQUE

Arrowhead Pattern—Straight Laid-In Insert the pattern thread in the successive plain weave sheds either before *or* after the background filling and keep consistent throughout pattern. The turns were accomplished on the face of the cloth. Be careful when doing this to keep the turns even so that no unsightly loops are left on the surface.
Block Pattern In the block design for the back of bag, the turns of the pattern filling were accomplished on the back side so that the surface of the fabric was smooth and without texture.

Prepare butterflies of your pattern color. Use individual butterflies for each pattern section. Also have your drawing ready. I had each square of the graph equal two warp ends and one filling pick. Dull

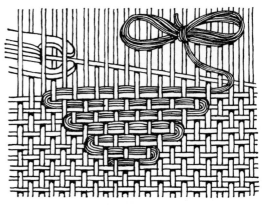

Arrow head pattern. "Straight laid-in" shows the turns on the face of the fabric.

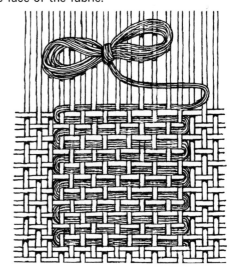

Block pattern. "Straight laid-in" shows the turns on the wrong side of the fabric.

olive is the background color for the back of the bag.

1. Weave in heading.	3. Weave ¾″ orange band.
2. Start with back hem.	4. ¼″ dull olive band.
Weave 1″ dark gold.	5. ⅜″ orange band.

6. ¾″ two orange blocks of laid-in. Open next shed, put in background filling. Beat down. With shed still open, count over to warp end where pattern begins, insert pattern butterfly from back of shed into open shed. Travel from right to left edge of pattern, bring butterfly out at back of shed. Beginning tail of butterfly can be turned around warp end at right edge of pattern. Do this for both orange blocks. Beat down, change sheds, put background in new shed. Beat, insert filling butterfly from back, traveling left to right. Bring out of shed at rear, beat down. Continue in this manner until block is complete. Cut pattern thread, loop around warp end at end of pattern.

7. ¾″ lemon yellow blocks—laid-in
8. 1¼″ orange blocks—laid-in
9. ½″ orange band
10. ⅜″ gold band
11. ⅜″ dull olive band
12. ¼″ gold band
13. ¼″ lemon yellow band
14. ⅛″ gold band
15. ⅜″ dull olive band
16. ⅛″ gold band
17. ⅜″ orange band
18. 1″ lemon yellow blocks—laid-in
19. 1″ orange blocks—laid-in
20. ¾″ lemon yellow blocks—laid-in
21. 1¼″ orange blocks—laid-in
22. ¾″ orange band
23. ⅜″ gold band
24. ½″ dull olive band—begins front of bag.
25. arrowhead and rosette motifs start here. 1½″ dull olive triangles—laid-in.

Background color is dark gold. Do laid-in as in step #6, except always bring pattern butterflies to top surface at pattern edge and insert from top so that a small "bump" appears where turn is made. Beginning and end of pattern thread are tucked in towards back of weaving.

26. 1″ gold rosettes—laid-in
27. ⅝″ orange squares—laid-in
28. 2 rows of 1″ lemon yellow triangles—laid-in
29. ⅜″ orange rosettes—laid-in
30. 1″ gold triangles—laid-in
31. 1″ lemon yellow triangles and ⅜″ orange dots (turn on the inside)—laid-in.
32. 1″ dull olive triangles—laid-in
33. ½″ 3 rows of orange laid-in, skip a shed in between so that laid-in always falls in same shed
34. ½″ orange band
35. ½″ same as step #33
36. 1½″ dull olive triangles—laid-in
37. 1″ dark gold hem.

FINISHING

1. Cut warp off loom, leaving warp ends about 2″ to 3″ long that can be tied, two together, or braided back so warp won't unravel.
2. If you want to line the bag, choose a medium-weight cotton twill, cut to size of bag less 2″.
3. Seam up sides of bag and lining. Insert lining. Catch stitch lining top to bag. Turn hem in, catch stitch to lining. If lining is omitted, catch stitch hem to bag.
4. To make the carrying braid: cut two lengths each of two colors to make four lengths, each 160″ long. Fold lengths in half and put around a chair post so they will be taut while being braided.

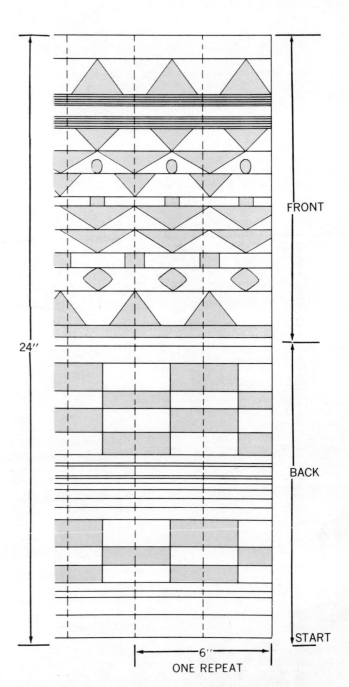

Greek bag pattern. Start Step 2 at bottom of diagram and work up. Two repeats are needed to obtain width of the bag. Shaded areas indicate laid-in pattern.

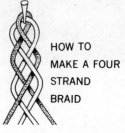

5. Adjust to proper length, sew to bag. Tassels, 4″ long, can be added at corners or smaller ones across entire bottom of bag. If no tassels are used, the braid may be continued across bottom of bag.

HOW TO MAKE A FOUR STRAND BRAID

The design of this tapestry was suggested by a beach scene and woven in various tapestry techniques. Shells and novelty yarns create the texture.

Other examples of handwoven fabrics are the Mexican plain weave upholstery and a window blind of mixed fibers and bamboo.

TAPESTRY TECHNIQUE

A tapestry can be pure ornamentation as in a wall hanging, but the techniques are also used to weave handbags, belts, bands, rugs, and covers for footstools and small pillows. The basic weave is the same as that used in the background of the rya rug—plain weave beaten down over a widely spaced warp, covering it so that only the filling yarn shows. Since tapestries are usually representational or abstract patterns, they cannot be woven selvedge to selvedge on the same pick, but in sections according to how design motifs and color fall. There are various techniques that provide for the joining of these sections or for a smooth transition from one section to another. As you will see, these techniques can also be used as design elements in the overall composition.

Before starting the tapestry it is essential to have a sketch of the design, known as a cartoon. Beginners should use a simple pattern. Keep the tapestry cartoon near at hand for easy checking—if convenient, attach it to the back of the warp. You could also paint the outlines of the design directly onto the warp. Working with simple areas gives you a chance to develop yarn and color effects.

Tapestry weaving is usually done with the face away from the weaver; however, it can be woven face up if in this way the weaver feels more control over the desired effect.

The loom used can be of either the harness or frame variety, although a true tapestry loom is more closely related to the frame loom.

Color and design are taken care of by the filling. This can be almost any yarn—from the finest silk to the heaviest roving, from the shiniest flat metallic to the dullest texture. The warp is chosen for strength since the heavy beating down of the filling puts much stress on it. Linen, hard-twist wool, and cotton (sett at 8 to 12 ends per inch) are the yarns most frequently used.

Although it is fascinating to use many varied yarns and colors in a tapestry, results just as interesting can be achieved by a creative blending of a few carefully selected yarns and colors. The change from

This tapestry design was influenced by the landscape of a Greek island, Santorini. Several tapestry techniques were used to achieve the textural effects, seen in detail below.

one type of yarn to another within the tapestry should not be too rapid or an unnatural buckling in the surface will develop. Sometimes this can be steamed out at the finishing, but it is unwise to depend on this.

Since ideally tapestry should be a personal statement by the weaver, the project offered here is a sampler warp on which to try out the techniques that follow.

TECHNIQUES

1. Slit Vertical opening where two areas come together. When the filling threads of both areas reach their boundaries, they turn on adjacent warp threads and reverse direction. The slit that results may be left open—in some cases to form part of the design —or sewn together. Sewing is done when the tapestry is completed and on the wrong side with no stitches visible on the right side. Strong fine thread is run through the loops at the slit, going from one side of slit to the other and drawing the edges together. When making a turn in the weaving, do not pull tightly on the filling or else the warp end, around which the turn is being made, will be pulled out of line leaving a gap.

2. Dovetailing Vertical joining of filling threads one from the right and one from the left, both turning around the same warp thread. This type of interlocking closes the space between sections and gives a vertical toothed pattern to the surface. The usual pattern of interlocking is 1 thread from each direction, but you could also use 2, 3, or 4 threads from each direction. Keep the number uniform in each section or an uneven effect will develop. The weaving must proceed at the same level or the joining will be askew. A slight ridge is made in the fabric at the point of dovetailing.

3. Interlocking Vertical joining of the filling threads from each direction by interlocking them between the warp ends before the filling threads reverse direction. Care must be taken that both filling threads are weaving in a straight line with each other and that a loose loop is not left at point of interlocking.

4. Diagonal Natural closing in a tapestry formed by diminishing the area of one color by a specified number of warp ends, and advancing the area of another color. This progression moves over one warp end with each pick—or more, depending on how steep the pitch of the diagonal will be. Vertical slits will form if the pitch is very steep.

SUGGESTED PROJECT

Below is a diagram for a sampler warp. The numbers correspond to the techniques described. The areas are left unshaded. Copy the drawing below, then color the areas as you wish.

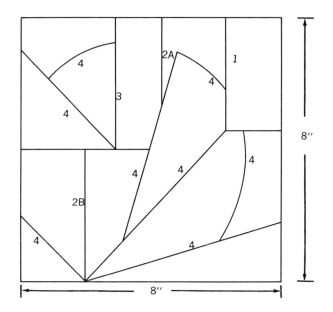

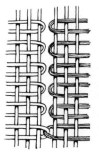

1 SLIT

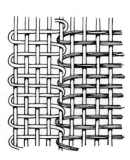

2A DOVETAILING

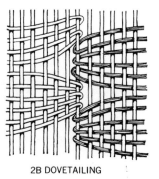

2B DOVETAILING

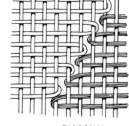

3 INTERLOCKING

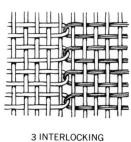

4 DIAGONAL

Suggested Materials **Warp** Linen or cotton warp yarn. Linen should be at least a 5 ply with a hard twist. Cotton can be 8/4's. All yarns designated as "rug warp" can be used.

Filling Experiment with yarns of different colors, weights and textures. Besides showing you the interesting effects you could plan into your tapestry, this experimenting will teach you where to make adjustments when using different weights of yarn so that the tapestry will lie smooth.

CALCULATIONS

sett 8 to 10 ends to the inch.
width on loom 8″
length ½ yd. plus loom allowance.
Continuous warp on the frame loom.

DESIGN

The first 8″ of the sampler are diagramed here. But, since you will have enough warp on your loom, you can repeat this diagram in different colors and yarns until you have woven the techniques to your satisfaction—or you can change the diagram. You may want to practice one technique more than another, or change the angle of the design in some areas. Also you may want to incorporate shapes, ideas, and techniques you have seen in other tapestries. These changes will increase your familiarity with the techniques and will make you aware of what shapes and effects are best in a tapestry. This is the first step in creating your own tapestry.

HELPFUL HINTS

1. Weave 1″ to 2″ plain weave headings at the beginning and end of your tapestry—rather loosely beaten in. These can be hemmed back later or taken out and a short fringe made.

2. A tapestry beater or ordinary household fork can be used to do the beating in individual sections. In some cases your fingers can help comb down the filling. Beating starts at point where filling entered shed and ends at point where filling exited. The filling should be in loosely enough to cover the warp without leaving loops on the surface after beating.

3. The filling is usually carried on small bobbins, specially made for tapestry weaving. The Gobelin bobbin and the Aubusson bobbin (called a flute) are shown here. The point of the Gobelin bobbin is used for beating down. I also use the butterflies and bobbins used for Argyle sock knitting.

GOBELIN BOBBIN

AUBUSSON FLUTE

4. Never carry threads over areas—cut and begin anew. To begin and end sections, put tail of filling thread around warp end at boundary and back into section under a couple of warp ends in same shed. All tails should be on the wrong side and can be clipped close at completion of tapestry. In cases where a bulky yarn does not permit this reentering, tails should be brought to the wrong side and darned in when the tapestry is off the loom.

5. Unless this is part of your design, selvedges and width of tapestry should be uniform throughout. Because of various weights and fiber contents involved in filling yarns and the weaving of shapes that distort the warp, a beginner may find the tapestry narrowing. To overcome this, darn a strong cord through both selvedges at intervals of 2″ to 5″. Stretch the tapestry to its intended width by pulling tightly on the cords. Tie the cords to both sides of the loom.

FINISHING

1. Machine stitch through the end rows of hem, unless you intend to make a fringe. The hem can be sewn to the tapestry with the sides left open so that dowels can be inserted and the tapestry hung.

2. Block before hemming. Attach the tapestry to a soft plywood board using nonrusting tacks or nails. Stretch it to the correct size, with corners square and edges even. Wet tapestry with warm water and let dry thoroughly before removing tacks.

3. Or, wet a terry towel in warm water, wring out, and place over section to be steamed. With a very hot iron, barely touch the towel. The full weight of the iron will not force as much steam through the tapestry and will only flatten the yarn. Allow the damp tapestry to dry slowly and thoroughly.

(Above) Purse with braided drawstring. Woven of thick linen roving in leno, double Mexican lace, and Spanish lace techniques. A lining of contrasting color is added.

(Opposite) Fine yarns may also be used in lace weaves, as in place mat at right. (Note that the place mat is woven in the lace technique only in specified areas.)

LACE WEAVES

Leno, Mexican, Spanish

Up to now we have concentrated on a heavy beat and a covered, or nearly covered, warp. Now to the opposite effect—an open structure achieved by various techniques all under the heading of "lace weaves." Three of these techniques—leno, Spanish lace, and Mexican lace—are used in the purses shown.

To create the open quality of lace, warp ends are pulled together by the filling or are twisted over each other. The warp must be strong to undergo the extra tension caused by the twisting. Since the twisted ends produce so much interest, it is better to keep the filling a solid color, one close to the warp color.

The different lace weaves can be used to decorate drapery or apparel fabrics, table linens, pillow covers, and shawls, or, on a large scale, screens or room divider panels.

SUGGESTED MATERIALS FOR PURSES

Warp Linen roving, ½ lb. per purse.
Filling Linen roving, ¼ lb. per purse.

For a different shade or texture, try white wrapping twine (24 ply) or a finer weight linen, using two or three strands together.

CALCULATIONS

Sett 5 ends per inch #10 reed sleyed every other dent. Selvedges are not doubled in dent, but placed in adjoining dents. Only one extra thread on either side for selvedge. Total number of ends, 62.

Width on Loom 12″

Length *Frame loom,* a continuous warp; *table or floor model,* 1 yd. plus loom allowance. The first 10″ to 12″ can be used for practice. On the frame loom, a narrow practice warp is recommended before putting on the purse warp.

Length of Purse #1 Per side, 12″ + 1″ hem.

Length of Purse #2 Per side, 12″ + 1″ hem.

Warp Plan Straight draw (see page 47).

TECHNIQUES

Leno

Leno is the most common lace weave and structurally the simplest. With a pick-up stick (see Glossary), pull the warp ends from the lower layer of the shed to the right, up and over an equal number of warp ends in the top layer. Leno is always worked from right to left for the first twist.

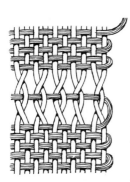 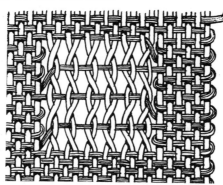

Leno weaves as worked from selvedge to selvedge (left). The ends are twisted to create open spaces, as worked in sections (right). Plain weave is built up around sections so that weaving proceeds evenly across the web.

In the following directions one end from the lower layer is twisted over one in the top layer, and worked across the entire web, as in the purses. Or, two or three ends can be twisted together using an equal number in both layers of the shed. Leno can also be woven in blocks, separated by sections of plain weave. Before you do these variations, put your pattern on graph paper. Each square should equal a given number of warp ends and filling picks, according to thickness of yarn and number of ends involved in a twist.

1. Plain weave, ending with a left to right shot of filling.
2. Beat in last pick of plain weave, change shed. Beat again, leave shed open. Put filling thread aside and take pick-up stick.
3. Start from right side, put the flat side of the stick under first end in lower shed. Lift end, move with it on stick to right of first upper end.
4. Slide stick with lower end on it over first upper end (this is the actual twist) and down under second lower end.

5. Pick up second lower end on stick, bring to right, up and over second upper end.
6. Move stick down to third lower end and continue in above manner.
7. When you finish the row, all the ends from the lower shed should be on the stick. Close shed, turn pick-up stick on its edge to form a new shed. Insert filling right to left. Return stick to level position to close shed.
8. With stick push down new filling as far as it will go, but don't force it. Remove stick. The twist has been locked into position by the filling.
9. Beat down again. Check that spaces formed by the twist are even all the way across.
10. Open plain weave shed, insert filling left to right. This gives an automatic twist to the ends. Continue steps 2 to 9 for more leno or return to plain weave.

Mexican Lace

This is a more elaborate form of leno. The twist here is also between the upper and lower layers of the shed, but the twisting order is uneven. This difference adds more curve to the warp ends, but it also adds more stress. Therefore, care should be exercised in beating or the ends may snap.

There is single Mexican lace and double Mexican lace—so called according to the number of ends twisted together.

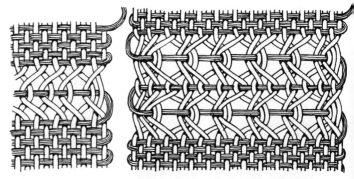

Single Mexican lace (left) worked across web. Note the curve in the twist is greater here than in leno. Three rows of double Mexican lace (right).

1. Plain weave on last pick from left to right.
2. Single twist—one end twisted over another except at selvedge. With pick-up stick go under the two

lower warp ends on right. Pull toward right of first upper end. Go over upper end, dip under next one in lower warp (end #3). Pick this up on stick also. Go over the next end at right in upper warp.

3. Continue picking up one under, move to right, over one upper.

4. At selvedge, one lower end goes over two upper ends. Close shed.

5. Stand stick on end, put filling through new shed, right to left.

6. Level pick-up stick and push filling down with it.

7. Beat down again with comb and beater, making sure that twist is even all the way across.

8. Change shed, put plain weave through left to right which automatically gives a second twist. Continue with Mexican lace or plain weave.

9. Double twist—two lower ends twisted over two upper ends. Follow above directions but begin at the right selvedge by pulling three lower ends to the right and over two upper ends. Go under next two in lower shed. Pull to right, go up and over two upper ends. Continue to selvedge where two lower ends go over three upper ends. Close shed.

10. Stand stick on end, insert filling in new shed right to left. Level stick, push down filling.

11. Change shed, beat again, put filling through left to right. Continue with Mexican lace or plain weave.

Spanish Lace

A subtler pattern than leno or Mexican, it is made by weaving over a fixed number of warp ends, then pulling them together into a group. This number is fixed by the size and shape of the pattern desired and the type of yarn used. The width of the opening between the groups is determined by how tightly

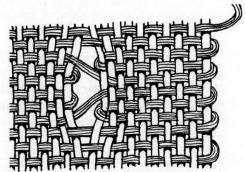

Spanish lace, worked in sections of ten ends.

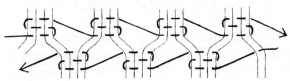

Diagram showing how to divide groups of ends for a staggered effect in Spanish lace.

the filling yarn is pulled back. However, you may choose not to pull the groups together in order to keep the small pattern that develops between them. The pattern can also be changed by altering the direction of the weaving. These pattern variations become more pronounced if the filling thread is much thicker and softer than the warp thread. The directions given are for four-end Spanish lace.

NOTE: The filling yarn should be in butterflies for easier manipulation between the small groups of warp ends. A pick-up stick is not used in making Spanish lace.

1. Plain weave on last pick, left to right.

2. Open next shed, pass filling through right to left under half the number of ends in your pattern. That is, if your pattern group is four ends, as here, then two ends would be in each shed.

3. Bring the filling to surface. Beat down with comb. The beater on a table or floor loom is not usually used for this weave.

4. Change sheds, insert filling left to right under the two warp ends. Pull the ends gently but firmly into a tight group. Beat down.

5. Change shed, insert filling right to left. Go under the two ends in first group *and also* two of the next group. Pull the first group together as you bring filling to surface. Beat down.

6. Change sheds, insert filling left to right under the two ends in the group #2 and come to the surface. Pull this group together and beat down.

7. Change sheds, insert filling right to left going under the two ends of group #2 and two ends of group #3. Pull group #2 together, beat down. As can be seen, you weave right, left, and right in one group before proceeding to next group.

8. Change sheds, continue in this manner.

9. After finishing a row, return to the right selvedge via plain weave, or weave the same pattern but count over left to right. In this case weave left, right, left before moving to the next group.

STEPS IN CONSTRUCTION

Combined here are the three lace weaves and the plain weave. The areas where they are used, plus their lengths in inches, are based on using linen roving in warp and filling.

Bamboo Handle Purse

1. 1½″ plain weave—includes hem
2. 3⅜″ double Mexican lace—
   3 rows of twists
   4 rows of spaces
3. ⅝″ plain weave
4. 1⅛″—1 row of single Mexican lace
5. ⅝″ plain weave
6. 2″—leno—3 rows of twists
   4 rows of spaces
7. ⅝″ plain weave
8. 1⅛″—1 row of single Mexican lace
9. 2″ plain weave
This completes one side of the purse. To weave the other side, reverse directions #9 through #1.

Drawstring Purse

1. 2¼″ plain weave, includes hem
2. 2″ leno, 3 rows twists, 4 rows of spaces
3. 1″ plain weave
4. 3⅜″ double Mexican lace, 3 rows of twists
   4 rows of spaces
5. 1″ plain weave
6. 1″ Spanish lace, 6 ends in group, weave 1st row, left to right weave 2nd row, right to left
7. ½″ plain weave
8. 2⅛″ Spanish lace, 4 ends in group, stagger each group
9. 2¼″ plain weave
This completes one side of the purse. To weave the other side, reverse directions #9 through #1.

Casement cloth, of linen roving and wrapping twine, using three techniques—the bottom section in Spanish lace, the middle Mexican lace, the top leno.

HELPFUL HINTS

1. The extra tension added to the warp ends during the twisting or pulling must be lessened or the warp ends will break. On the floor or table loom release the back ratchet as soon as you feel the warp tightening too much. On the frame loom, insert additional tension sticks to top and bottom of loom as the warp is wound around it. Then when you make the lace weave, these sticks can be removed to lessen tension and then reinserted, if necessary, for plain weave.

2. You must start the lace technique with the first selvedge thread on the right in the upper shed if you are working from selvedge to selvedge.

3. Have the filling in butterflies, on stick shuttles, or on very small boat shuttles in order to get it easily through the picked-up shed.

4. In working from selvedge to selvedge, be sure the filling is not pulled in too tightly. Lace areas tend to draw in, but are also somewhat elastic and will steam and block out to the required width.

5. To beat down, use pick-up stick, comb, or in some cases the beater. Spanish lace is easily pushed down with the fingers or a very narrow pick-up stick.

6. A white paper placed behind the warp will help you see the ends better.

7. Count, to be sure you have the correct number of ends on pick-up stick.

FINISHING

1. Overhand stitch at beginning and end of purse before removing warp from loom.

2. Block and press with steam iron for even selvedges.

3. Cut lining to size of purse, less hem. Slip stitch to purse.

4. Fold hem of plain weave over lining. Catch stitch to lining.

5. Purse with drawstring—Seam up sides only to the hem so that the drawstring can be inserted at the side into the casing formed by the hem. Make a braid 80″ long, as shown on page 69, to pull through hem casing. Tie ends of drawstring together after pulling through.

6. Purse with bamboo handle—Seam up sides and attach wooden or bamboo handle.

Purse with bamboo handles, woven of linen roving in the Mexican lace and leno techniques.

STOLE, PILLOW COVERS

Simple Weaves for the 4-Harness Loom

In the preceding pages you learned how simple techniques can lead to beautiful items of practical or aesthetic value. There is still much more that could be experimented with on a frame loom or using two sheds on a harness loom. Eventually, however, you will want to do some weaving on a larger loom that offers more structural and design possibilities. Therefore, the remaining pages are devoted to projects that will initiate you into weaving on a 4-harness loom.

I strongly recommend that the first item you weave on the 4-harness loom is a sample warp based on the weaves mentioned on page 45. This will acquaint you with the relationship between weave draft, drawing-in draft, and tie-up of treadles and order of treadling—or, as on a table loom, the order of pushing down the levers. The chain drafts are for the rising shed loom.

Following are directions for three small projects. They include pillow covers and a stole. The weave draft is not illustrated. The warp plan, or drawing-in draft, is a straight draw in all cases. The chain draft, with instructions for both table and floor loom, is indicated by each project. Although the 4-harness loom was used in all cases, the drafts can be adapted for looms with more harnesses.

Pillow cover woven in a combination of twill and plain weaves with a multicolored filling of textured yarns.

Small pillow cover of red and gold yarns, woven in plain weave on a 4-harness loom. Gold metallic thread is used to highlight the center bands.

Lightweight stole with fringe, in a twill weave. Note the off-center stripe in the warp.

LIGHTWEIGHT STOLE

Stripe Pattern in Warp

Suggested Materials for 72″ stole. 2/17′s weaving worsted. Turquoise—½ lb.—for both warp and filling; 2 oz. black, for warp only.

Sett 20 ends per inch—#10 reed sleyed 2 per dent. Total number of ends, 400 + 8 for selvedge (4 on each side).

Width in Reed 20″.

Length of Warp 2 yds. + loom allowance.

Warping Order 50 T, 12 B, 10 T, 48 B, 15 T, 15 B, 8 T, 6 B, 244 T.

KEY T = Turquoise B = Black

Warp Plan Straight draw, single in heddles.

Filling Solid turquoise used singly.

Weave $\frac{2}{2}$ twill. Treadles are tied up to harnesses indicated. Treadle order is 1–4 repeated for the entire stole.

Finishing Cut off loom. Fray out a 3½″ fringe at each end. Separate fringe into small groups of about 15 to 20 ends and knot close to woven fabric so picks are secured in place. Wash in mild soap and warm water.

CHAIN DRAFT FOR LIGHTWEIGHT STOLE

TREADLE #

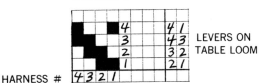

LEVERS ON TABLE LOOM

HARNESS #

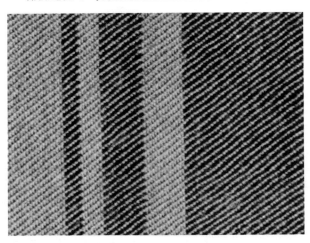

Detail of stole showing twill weave.

SMALL PILLOW COVER

Bands of Pattern in Contrasting Color Yarn and Metallic Yarn

Suggested Materials 2/20's weaving worsted. Completed size is 15″ x15″. 4 oz. gold and 4 oz. red for both warp and filling; 1 oz. gold metallic giumpe yarn, for filling only.

Sett 15 ends per inch, #15 reed sleyed 1 per dent. Total number of ends, 255 + 4 for selvedge (2 on each side).

Width in Reed 17″.

Length of Warp 1 yd. + loom allowance.

Warping Order 1 gold, 1 red.

Warp Plan Straight draw, single in heddles.

Filling Back of pillow is solid red. Front is a pattern of wide bands, randomly arranged in gold and red and alternating with ⅜″ wide bands of solid red filling. The arrangement of the predominantly gold bands is as follows, after 17″ of solid red filling:

BAND #1	BAND #2	BAND #4	BAND #
2 G ⎱ X 2	2 G	2 G + M	2 G
2 R ⎰	2 R	2 R ⎱ X 2	2 R
2 R	3 G	1 G + M ⎰	1 G
3 G	1 R ⎱ X 2	1 G + M	4 R
2 R	1 G ⎰	3 R	1 G ⎱ X
1 G	I G	2 G + M ⎱ X 3	2 R ⎰
	1 R	2 R	2 G
	2 R ⎱ X 2	3 G + M	2 R
	2 G ⎰	1 G + M ⎱ X 2	1 G
		3 R ⎰	3 R
		3 G + M	4 G
		1 R	1 R
			1 G

(KEY: R = red, G = gold, M = metallic, X = times)

Band #3 Like band #1 but with metallic thread added in with every gold pick.

Band #5 Like band #2 but with metallic thread added in with every gold pick.

Band #7 Like band #6 minus last 2 picks and reading column from bottom to top.

Band #8 Like band #6 minus last 2 picks and first 2 picks.

Band #9 Like band #6 minus last 6 picks.
Weave Plain weave beaten down fairly heavy.
Chain See page 48 for plain weave on a 4-harness loom.
Finishing Cut off loom. Run a line of machine stitching at both cut ends of cloth to keep filling from fraying. Wash in soap and warm water. Fit to pillow size and seam two selvedge sides on wrong side of cloth. Invert and insert pillow. Sew opening.

MULTICOLORED PILLOW

Bands of Textured Yarn

Suggested Materials 2-ply wool (suiting weight), Nordic rya yarn, knitting worsted, wool *bouclé* (or any heavy textured yarn). Amounts given are for finished pillow size 19″ x 14″.
Reddish-Purple, Brown, Wine, Red (2-ply wool)—2 oz. of each for warp.
Brilliant Purple Nordic rya yarn—4 oz. for filling.
Royal Blue knitting worsted—2 oz. for filling.
Deep Turquoise wool *bouclé*—2 oz. for filling.
Sett 20 ends per inch—# 10 reed sleyed 2 per dent. Total number of ends, 400 + 4 for selvedge (2 on each side).
Width in Reed 20″.
Length of Warp 1 yd. + loom allowance.
Warping Order 1 red, 1 brown, 1 purple, 1 wine.
Warp Plan straight draw, 2 ends in each heddle.
Filling back and front of pillow cover are the same. After doing one side, start the second side with 1″ (1B, 1T) and end with 2″ P.

CHAIN DRAFT FOR MULTICOLORED PILLOW

TREADLE #

HARNESS #   4 3 2 1   LEVERS ON TABLE LOOM

NOTE: The A and B designations in the chain draft always denote the plain weave tie-up of the treadles.

Weave Plain weave in purple sections and in blue and purple sections; broken twill in the turquoise and blue sections and the solid blue in these areas.

Treadles A and B are tied up for plain weave. 1, 4, 2, 3, for a $\frac{2}{2}$ broken twill. Follow both weaves in consecutive order, but mix weaves together when color calls for it.
Finishing Follow directions as given for red and gold pillow cover.

(KEY: B = blue, T = turquoise, P = purple, X = times) Where inches are not indicated, measurement is in picks.

COL. 1	COL. 2
½″ P	½″ P
1″ (1 B, 1T)	2 B
1″ P	1 P ⎫
1 B ⎫	1 B ⎬ X 2
1 T ⎬ X 2	1 T ⎭
2 B	1 B
½″ P	½″ P
1 B ⎫	1 B ⎫
1 T ⎬ X 4	1 T ⎬ X 3
5 B	5 B
1 B ⎫	1 B ⎫
1 T ⎬ X 3	1 T ⎬ X 2
8 B	3 B
1 B ⎫	½″ P
1 T ⎬ X 3	4 B
	2 P

COL. 3	COL. 4
1 B ⎫	2 B
1 T ⎬ X 4	1 B ⎫
1 B	1 T ⎬ X 4
2 P	4 B
1 B ⎫	1 B ⎫
1 T ⎬ X 2	1 T ⎬ X 3
7 B	1 B
1 B ⎫	½″ P
1 T ⎬ X 3	2 B
1 B	3 P
½″ P	1 B ⎫
2 B	1 T ⎬ X 2
2 P	1 B
1 B ⎫	1½″ P
1 T ⎬ X 2	

Poncho of medium weight wool with braided tie at neckline. A very popular garment of South America, this is a straight piece of weaving, and requires no sewing.

APPAREL FABRICS

Wider Fabrics Using Variations on Weaves

After you have become accustomed to weaving on a loom more complex than the frame variety, you will undoubtedly begin to think of weaving larger projects and will want to try out variations on the simple weave structures we have used thus far. Fabrics that seem to fall into this class are those woven as yardage for suits, skirts, dresses, and coats.

Simple weaves are very well suited to apparel fabrics and do not conflict with the color arrangement nor do they overshadow the textured yarns that enhance many of these fabrics. The "homespun look" of much of our commercially produced sport and casual fabrics is in reality our old friend, the plain weave. Another popular weave found in apparel fabrics is the twill weave which produces a cloth that is elegant, drapes well, and has a lustrous surface.

Tweed coat dress of woolen fabric in a plain weave.

Weaving tweeds is a natural for the handloom. These tweeds can be almost any combination from related hues subtly arranged as in the poncho to an effect as bold as the "salt and pepper" in the coat dress.

In the projects given here, I obtained the color effect I wanted by using two threads as one in the warp. In these instances the warp is threaded double in the heddles.

As before, a small sample warp is suggested so that you can see the result before investing in yarns for the yardage. Also ideas may develop that did not occur to you originally.

Detail of poncho showing weave and color arrangement. Warp and filling threads are used double for weight and color effect.

Lightweight yarns are best for suiting and dresses; the heavier ones should be saved for coating. The picks per inch should be the same as the ends per inch, or less. In finishing, the cloth will shrink sufficiently to give a fabric that is firm but pliable enough to sew.

For weavers not handy with a needle, there are woven garments that require a minimum of or no sewing. One such item is the poncho described here. This is an idea transported to us from our South American neighbors and very popular for college, country, and leisure wear.

In weaving these wide fabrics be sure to throw your shuttle with enough force to send it to the other side of the loom; if not, it may fall through the warp shed to the bottom. Also take care not to pull the selvedges in too tightly since a looser selvedge shrinks in better. The beat should be even throughout the fabric so that streaks will not result from where picks have been suddenly placed in too loosely or too tightly.

MEDIUM-WEIGHT PONCHO WITH SUBTLE STRIPE EFFECT

Suggested Materials 2-ply wool (suiting weight), 3-ply (medium-weight) rug wool, knitting worsted. **NOTE:** The poncho was woven for a person of medium to tall height and falls slightly above the knee. Amounts given are for this size.

reddish purple ¾ lb. (2-ply suiting wool)—warp

brown ¾ lb. (2-ply suiting wool)—warp

wine 1 lb. (2-ply suiting wool)—warp and filling

red 1 lb. (2-ply suiting wool)—warp and filling

rust ¾ lb. (3-ply medium-weight rug wool)—filling

burnt orange ½ lb . (knitting worsted)—filling

magenta ¾ lb. (knitting worsted)—filling

Sett 20 ends per inch—#10 reed sleyed 2 per dent. Total number of ends, 900 + 8 for selvedge (4 on each side.)
Width in Reed 45″.
Length of Warp 2½ yards + loom allowance.
Warping Order 1 red, 1 brown, 1 purple, 1 wine.
Warp Plan Straight draw—2 ends in each heddle.

Filling Wine, red, rust, burnt orange and magenta.

11″ red and rust (used as 1 pick) —including 1½″ hem	⅝″ red and rust
	⅜″ burnt orange
½″ burnt orange (2 strands used as 1 pick)	⅞″ red and rust
¾″ red and rust	¼″ burnt orange
⅜″ burnt orange	4″ red and rust
⅜″ red and rust	¼″ burnt orange
1⅛″ burnt orange	⅜″ red and rust
⅝″ red and rust	⅝″ burnt orange
2½″ magenta and wine (used as 1 pick)	⅜″ red and rust
⅜″ red and rust	11½″ magenta and wine
⅝″ burnt orange	This finishes one side of poncho.

For the back side, continue until magenta and wine section measures 23″ in all. Then proceed up the column back to the hem. The slit for the head begins at the start of the magenta and wine section and continues upward for 15″. To make the slit, find the center of the warp and then work two shuttles simultaneously, one going from the right selvedge to the slit, and the other from the slit to the left selvedge. The slit opening should have an even edge. Do not pull at the edge threads with the filling or the slit will appear distorted.

Weave Broken twill in red and rust sections, plain weave in burnt orange and magenta sections.

Finishing Wash in mild soap and lukewarm water. Hem. For the tie, make a 3-strand braid of the

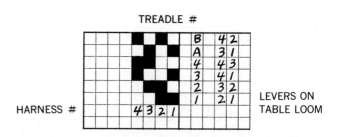

CHAIN DRAFT FOR PONCHO

NOTE: The A and B designations in the chain draft always denote the plain weave tie-up of the treadles.

various colors used in the warp. Knot the ends leaving a 2″ fringe. Pull through cloth, 6½″ up from the bottom of slit and on either side of slit, being careful not to break any ends or picks. If you do not wish to have braided tie, make the slit about 6″ shorter.

TWEED FABRIC FOR A COAT DRESS

Suggested Materials 2/20's worsted, 2/17's worsted, 2-ply wool (suiting weight). French novelty wool yarn, cotton novelty slub yarn.

NOTE: the coat dress takes 4¾ yds. of 35″ wide fabric for a size 14. Figure your yardages according to your correct size and the type of garment you wish to make. Use this finished length in your calculations to find the dressed length; be careful to allow for the take-up and, in the width, the draw-in.

1) ½ lb. light wine 2/20's worsted—warp

2) ½ lb. deep wine, 2/20's worsted—warp

3) ¼ lb. off-white 2/17's worsted—warp

4) ½ lb. black/white cotton novelty slub yarn—warp

5) ½ lb. black/white French novelty wool yarn—warp

6) 2¼ lbs. white/wine 2-ply wool (suiting weight)—warp and filling

Sett 20 ends per inch—#10 reed sleyed 2 per dent. Total number of ends, 800 + 8 for selvedge (4 on each side).

Width in Reed 40″.

Length of Warp 5 yds. + loom allowance.

Warping Order 1,5,6,4,3,2, repeat—refer to yarn list above.

Warp Plan Straight draw, every third heddle has two ends in it.

Filling Solid white/wine 2-ply wool.

Weave Plain weave.

Chain For plain weave—see page 48.

Finishing Machine-stitch beginning and end of yardage so picks will not fray out. Wash in mild soap and warm water. Let dry and steam press.

Detail of coat dress fabric. The character of the plain weave is changed completely by the yarn combinations in both warp and filling.

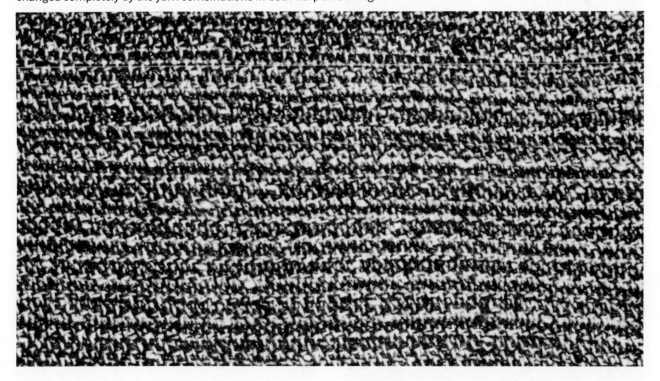

UPHOLSTERY FABRICS

Heavier Fabrics Using Complex Warp Plan and Weaves

When a more complex warp plan is used, the opportunities for pattern and textural effects expand limitlessly.

Up to now we have been using the straight draw warp plan on the 4-harness loom, but used here for the upholstery fabric is a variation of a warp plan for the weave commonly called "honeycomb." Instead of using the chain draft usually associated with this weave, I tried variations until I got the fabrics I wanted for my dining room chairs. By referring to the photographs shown, you can see the entirely different weaves obtained in the fabric. The chains were based on plain weave and the warp-faced twill weave, but a combination weave resulted from the mixing of these two chains.

The honeycomb warp plan tends to give long floats of filling on the reverse side. Because of this the fabric would not lend itself to uses that expose both sides nor to those where the floats could be easily caught or pulled. It lends itself perfectly, however, as a covering for a chair seat or footstool where the reverse side would not show. However, whenever the reverse side is exposed—as it would be in a purse, for example—a lining should be added.

When weaving upholstery, it is necessary to have strong yarns and a weave that will stand much wear. Also, construction must be tight so that the threads will not shift. A tight construction is one in which the sett is high, or dense, and the beat is heavy, making the number of picks per inch proportionately high. A tight construction is also necessary so that the padding of the chair seat, for example, will not show through as the fabric is being stretched to fit.

The five swatches shown here and on the opposite page are all upholstery fabrics made on the same warp. Their variations result from differences in weave structure and color placement. The red swatch is in plain weave with a solid red filling. The other four are in combination weaves with mixed colors in the filling.

Honeycomb Ridged Effect   Honeycomb Textural Effect

The honeycomb warp plan produces a heavy fabric that gives a subtle ridge effect caused by dips that travel the length of the warp, as shown on left; or a textural effect caused by small raised dots as shown on right.

On the previous page is illustrated a fabric to be used as seat covers for chairs. The finished width is the width of the chair seats, plus the allowance needed for tucking under.

UPHOLSTERY FABRIC FOR DINING ROOM CHAIRS

Suggested Materials 3- or 4-ply rug wool. If lighter weight yarn is used, it should be set very dense in the reed, or two or three threads used as one. For the chair illustrated, a piece of fabric 28″ x 23″ is needed.

royal blue	4 oz. warp
bright purple	4 oz. warp
deep teal	4 oz. warp

WARP PLAN FOR HONEYCOMB WEAVE

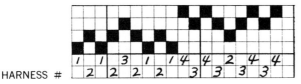

HARNESS #

Ridged Effect

deep rose	4 oz.	filling yarn
dull violet	4 oz.	filling yarn
red	2 oz.	filling yarn

Sett 12 per inch. Total number of ends, 384 + 8 for selvedges (4 on each side).
Width in Reed 32″ wide.
Length of Warp 23″ + loom allowance.
Warping Order 1 Purple, 1 Royal Blue, 1 Teal repeated throughout.
Warp Plan Single in heddles

Filling 2 Dull Violet, 1 Deep Rose, 1 Red, 1 Deep Rose repeated throughout.
Chain Draft The order of treadling is: A, B, 1, 2, 1, repeat. The corresponding levers would be pushed on a table loom.

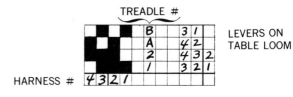

HARNESS #

Finishing Machine stitch beginning and end of fabric. Wash in mild soap and luke-warm water.

Textural Effect

teal	6 oz. filling yarn
brown	6 oz. filling yarn

Sett width in reed, total number of ends, length of warp, warping order, warp plan—as for Ridged Effect at left.

Filling 4 Brown, 4 Blue repeated throughout.
Chain Draft The order of treadling is: 1, 2, 1, 2, A, B, A, B, 3, 4, 3, 4, A, B, A, B, repeat. The corresponding levers would be pushed on a table loom.

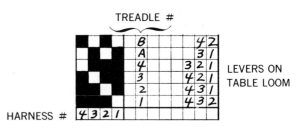

HARNESS #

Finishing as for Ridged Effect at left.

COLONIAL OVERSHOT

The pattern structure called "colonial overshot" is an example of a weave that looks more complex than it actually is. You will eventually be able to analyze such fabrics and see with what simplicity and logic they have been constructed.

Called "colonial overshot" because we associate it with our early settlers, this type of weaving is also known in Scandinavia, the Balkans, and Greece— but it was not known in England until recently, so it is doubtful that it was brought over here by the Pilgrims. Even so, it remains a true heritage from the early founders of this country. It seems to have been an especially favored product of our colonial weavers and examples of it, particularly in coverlets, are found in many museums and early American restorations.

The weave is in three colors—the pattern, the background, and the pattern and background combined.

The overshot forms the pattern; it skips over the ground weave and creates a pattern of short floats. The yarn used for the pattern should be soft, but heavier than the background filling so that it can be beaten down well and still stand out boldly. The background is formed by the warp and filling— usually of the same thread count. The third color is formed by the pattern interweaving with the background.

The background is a plain weave. The pattern weave is based usually on twill blocks. That is 1,2 weave together, 2,3,3,4, and 4,1. The way in which the loom is threaded brings areas of these blocks together to form the pattern. Between every pick of pattern filling, there is one pick of plain weave. In the warp plan an odd number has to follow an even number since this way we can be sure that the plain weave will be constructed correctly.

The directions given are for the pillow cover, 20″ x 12″. If you wish to adapt this pattern for the coverlet, take the pattern motif marked on the warp plan and repeat it enough times to fulfill the width of your coverlet; then add the border pattern.

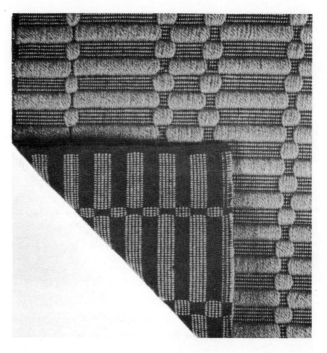

(Above) "Monk's Belt," a simple adaptation of overshot, showing a section of reverse side. (Below) Detail of traditional coverlet in the Double Bowknot pattern, wool and cotton, woven in Ohio in 1867. (Courtesy The Smithsonian Institute)

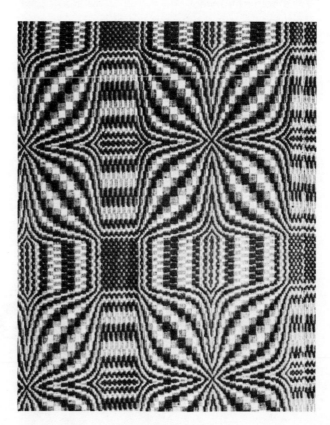

On the same threading two pattern variations are possible. Pillow cover in the "Lover's Knot" pattern above, and the bedspread shown on the opposite page were developed from above sample warps.

LOVER'S KNOT PILLOW

Suggested Materials 15/3's mercerized cotton and 2/7's homespun wool.

Rose 15/3 cotton 6 oz. warp and filling background.
Red 2/7 Nordic homespun pattern filling 6 oz.

Sett 20 per inch. Total number of ends, 420 + 4 for selvedge (2 on each side).

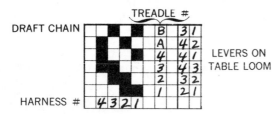

Width in Reed 21" reed.
Length of Warp 26" + loom allowance.
Warping Order Solid rose cotton.
Warp Plan As illustrated in draft—single in heddles.

Filling Rose cotton on plain weave, red wool on pattern weave.

Hem Start with 1" plain weave. *Do not forget* that between every pick of pattern listed there is one of plain weave.

Treadling Order

BORDER	CENTER MOTIF		SMALL MOTIF
*2—5x	4—3x	1—3x	1—3x
1—4x	3—3x	2—3x	2—3x
2—2x	2—3x	3—5x	1—3x
1—4x	1—3x	4—4x	
2—5x	2—2x	3—2x	
		†4—2x	

*Treadle #
†From here, work back to first motif pick to complete circle.
X = Times

Repeat center motif twice and border once to complete the front. The back may be all plain weave or the same pattern as front. **Finishing** Seam three sides, right sides together. Invert and insert pillow. Sew top seam, making sure to fold hem under.

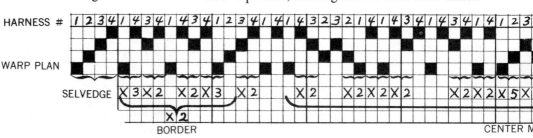

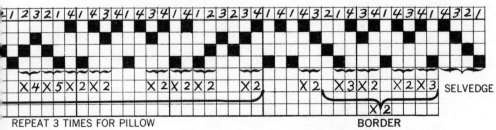

WARP PLAN

X4X5X2X2   X2X2X2   X2   X2 X3X2 X2X3   SELVEDGE

X2

REPEAT 3 TIMES FOR PILLOW   BORDER

A continuous draft for the "Lover's Knot" pillow.

glossary

Apron The canvas that attaches the apron bars to either the warp beam or cloth beam.

Apron bars Thin, strong, wood or metal rods to which the warp is attached at the front and back of loom.

Back beam The stationary upper beam at back of loom directly over the warp beam. Helps to keep the warp at an even tension by giving it a smooth surface to glide over. Also called whip roll.

Beaming Winding the warp onto the warp beam under tension.

Beater The movable frame that holds the reed. Pulling it forward pushes the filling into place in the warp. Also called batten.

Bobbin Filling thread is wound around this before it is inserted into the shuttle. Also called quill, or spool.

Breast beam Stationary top beam at front of loom over which the woven cloth passes to the cloth beam below.

Butterfly A hand-bobbin arrangement of filling yarn, used without a holder and made by winding the yarn around the fingers in a figure eight.

Castle The central main structure of the loom that supports the harnesses.

Chain A series of continuous loops (similar to a crochet chain) made in the warp to temporarily shorten its length; for easier handling from the warping device to the loom and to prevent tangling.

Chain draft A plan that indicates which harnesses to raise and in what order to raise them.

Chain-spacer Crochet-like loops made around the warp ends in a frame loom before weaving begins, to keep warp ends evenly spaced.

Cloth beam The rotating lower front beam of loom on which the finished cloth is rolled as it is woven.

Counterbalanced loom A loom with a sinking shed. See sinking shed.

Cross Formed as warp ends cross in alternate succession around pegs on a warping board or reel. It simplifies the threading of the loom by keeping the ends in order and free from tangles. Also called lease.

Dent The space between two bars in a reed. Reeds come in various sizes according to the number of dents per inch they carry.

Draft A drawing of a weave pattern on graph paper showing its threading and weaving order.

Drawing-in Threading the warp ends through the heddle eyes and the reed dents.

Dressing the loom Preparing the loom for weaving.

Ends Individual lengths of warp threads.

Fibers Synthetic or natural hair-like filaments which when spun together form thread or yarn.

Filling The yarn that is interwoven with the warp ends. Also called weft.

Harness Two bars hung in the center of the loom and between which the heddles are hung.

Heading A narrow band of heavy yarn, string, or rags woven in at the beginning of the fabric.

Heddle Flat metal strip, string, or wire with a loop or eye in its center that is suspended between the harnesses. Holds the warp threads in position.

Heddle cords Long loops of cord attached to the heddle rod of a frame loom. The alternate warp ends pass through these to form one of the sheds.

Heddle eye Loop or opening in the center of heddle through which the warp ends are threaded according to pattern chosen.

Heddle rod The bar that carries the looped cord heddles on frame, tapestry, and stick looms.

Jack loom A loom with a rising shed. See rising shed.

Lams Horizontal levers between the harnesses and treadles and attached to both.

Lease See cross.

Lease rods Flat, thin, smooth sticks inserted into the warp on either side of the cross to keep the cross in order while beaming and threading the loom. Also called lease stick.

Levers The bars on table looms which raise the harnesses when pressed.

Loom A frame for holding the warp ends under tension so weaving can take place.

Mordants The chemical compounds used to set color.

Pick A single passage of filling thread through the shed. Also called shot.

Pick-up stick A thin, flat, beveled stick with a pointed end. Used as an aid in making extra shed openings for pattern weaving. 1″–2″ wide.

Piecing Starting a new thread where an old one has ended. Usually means the overlapping of the threads or rags used in the filling.

Pile The strands or loops of filling yarn that are so woven as to be raised above the surface of the cloth. Short pile is sometimes called flossa.

Plain weave The most basic weave formed by raising every even warp end over every odd filling shot and every odd end over every even shot. Also called tabby.

Ply The number of single threads that have been twisted together in a length of thread.

Quill A paper tube on which the filling is wound for insertion in a boat shuttle.

Raddle A toothed frame used to spread the warp while it is being beamed. Also called spreader.

Ratchet A wheel with notches or teeth, fastened to ends of warp and cloth beams to hold proper tension and to prevent unrolling.

Reed A comblike device set in the beater to space warp ends according to plan and to beat the filling down.

Reed hook A device with a hook at one end, used to pull the warp ends through the heddle eyes and reed dents.

Rising shed A shed opening made by the raising of alternate warp threads. (See Jack loom.)

Roving A soft, rope-like form of fibers from which yarns are made.

Rya A knotted rug with a long cut pile.

Selvedge Warpwise edge of the cloth.

Sett The number of warp ends per inch.

Shed The V-shaped opening formed by the raising or lowering of warp ends, through which passes the shuttle carrying the filling thread.

Shot See pick.

Shuttle The instrument that carries the filling threads.

Singles One continuous length of twisted yarn that has been spun from fibers.

Sinking shed A shed opening made by the lowering of alternate warp threads. See counterbalanced loom.

Skein Loosely wound yarn in a continuous strand. Also called hank.

Sleying Threading the warp through the dents in the reed.

Spinning Twisting of fibers to make a continuous strand of thread.

Tabby See plain weave.

Take-up The contraction of yarn caused by the interlacing of warp and filling.

Tapestry beater A comb or fork used in a frame loom to beat down the filling.

Tension The degree of tightness to which the warp is stretched on the loom.

Tension stick A thin flat stick inserted into the warp in a frame loom to adjust the tension.

Tie-up The planned sequence in which the harnesses are attached to the treadles of a floor loom.

Treadles Foot pedals that are attached to the harnesses on floor looms and raise or lower them.

Twill A basic weave in which the filling forms a diagonal pattern.

Warp The threads running lengthwise in a loom and through which the filling threads are passed to form the cloth.

Warp beam The rotating lower back beam around which the unwoven warp is wound and stored.

Warp-end bar The rod at the back of the frame loom around which a continuous warp is wound and spaced.

Warp ends See ends.

Warp plan Indication of the threading order of the warp through the heddles. Also called drawing-in draft and threading draft.

Warping board Wooden frame with spaced pegs around which the warp is measured and wound.

Warping reel A large barrel-like revolving wheel around which the warp is measured and wound. Also called a warping drum.

Weave draft The draft that indicates the pattern of the weave.

Web Piece of woven cloth.

Weft See filling.

Woof See filling.

books

ALBERS, Anni. *On Weaving.* Middletown, Conn., Wesleyan Univ. Press 1965.
AMSDEN, Charles A. *Navaho Weaving—Its Technique and History.* Santa Ana, Calif., The Fine Arts Press, 1934.
ATWATER, Mary M. *The Shuttle-craft Book of American Hand-weaving;* rev. ed., New York, N.Y., Macmillan, 1956.
BIRD, Junius. *Paracas Fabrics and Nazca Needlework.* technical analysis by Louisa Bellinger. Phila., Pa., National Publishing Co., 1954.
BIRRELL, Verla. *The Textile Arts: A Handbook of Fabric Structure and Design Processes.* New York, N.Y., Harper and Bros., 1959.
BLACK, Mary E. *New Key to Weaving.* Milwaukee, Wis., Bruce Publishing Co., 1957.
BLUMENAU, Lili. *The Art and Craft of Handweaving.* New York, N.Y., Crown Publishers, Inc., 1955.
BROOKLYN BOTANICAL GARDENS, *Dye Plants & Dyeing, A Handbook.* 1000 Washington Avenue, Brooklyn, New York.
BROWN, Harriette J. *Handweaving for Pleasure and Profit.* New York, N.Y., Harper and Bros., 1952.
CHERRY, Eve. *Teach Yourself Handweaving.* Roy Publishers, New York, N.Y., 1957.
CHRISTOPHER, F. J. *Hand-loom Weaving.* rev. ed., Hackensack, N.J., Wehman Bros., 1961.
CONLEY, Emma. *Vegetable Dyeing.* Penland, N.C., Penland School of Crafts.
D'HARCOURT, Raoul, and others. *Textiles of Ancient Peru and Their Techniques.* Washington, D.C., Univ. of Washington Press, 1962.
FREY, Berta. *Designing and Drafting for Handweavers.* New York, N.Y., Macmillan, 1958.
HOOPER, Luther. *Weaving With Small Appliances—Book I—The Weaving Board.* London, Eng., Sir I. Pitman & Sons, Ltd., 1922–25.
OELSNER, G. H. *A Handbook of Weaves.* rev. ed., by Samuel S. Dale. New York, N.Y., Dover Publications, Inc., 1961.
OVERMAN, Ruth, and Lula Smith. *Contemporary Handweaving.* Ames, Iowa, Iowa State College Press, 1958.
PLATH, Iona. *Handweaving.* New York, N.Y., Scribner, 1964.
THORPE, Heather G. *A Handweaver's Workbook.* New York, N.Y., Macmillan, 1956.
TIDBALL, Harriet. *Contemporary Tapestry.* Distributed by Craft and Hobby Book Service; Copyright by Shuttle-craft Guild, Big Sur, Calif., 1964.
TOD, Osma G. *The Joy of Handweaving.* 2nd ed., Princeton, N.J., Van Nostrand, 1964.
TOVEY, John. *The Technique of Weaving.* London, Eng., B. T. Batsford, Ltd., New York, N.Y., Reinhold Publishing Co., 1965.
WASSIF, Forman-Wiss. *Tapestries From Egypt.* London, Eng., Paul Hamlyn, 1961.
WATSON, William. *Textile Design and Color.* 6th ed., London, Eng., Longmans Green & Co., 1954.
WEIBEL, Adele Coulin. *Two Thousand Years of Textiles.* New York, N.Y., Pantheon Books, 1952.

periodicals

American Fabrics Magazine	Craft Horizons	Handweaver and Craftsman	The Shuttle Craft Guild
24 East 38th Street	16 East 52nd Street	220 Fifth Avenue	Route 1, Box 204 B
New York, **New York** 10016	New York, **New York** 10022	New York, **New York** 10001	Lansing, **Michigan** 48906

book services

Craft & Hobby Book Service	Museum Books, Inc.
Dept. HW	48 East 43rd Street
Big Sur, **California** 93920	New York, **New York** 10017

SUPPLIERS

yarn

The Yarn Depot	Bartlett Mills	The Mannings
545 Sutter St.	Harmony, **Maine**	East Berlin, **Pennsylvania** 17316
San Francisco, **California** 94102		
	Thomas Hodgson & Sons, Inc.	
William Condon & Sons	Concord, **New Hampshire**	Charles Y. Butterworth
65 Queen St. P.O. Box 129		2222 East Susquehanna Ave.
Charlottetown, P.E. Island, **Canada**	Home Yarns Co.	Philadelphia 25, **Pennsylvania**
	1849 Coney Island Ave.	
Contessa Yarns	Brooklyn, **New York** 11230	
Dept. HW		Conlin Yarns
P.O. Box 37	Fiber Yarn Co.	P.O. Box 11812
Lebanon, **Connecticut** 06249	840 6th Ave.	Philadelphia, **Pennsylvania** 19128
	New York, **New York** 10001	
House of Kleen·	Lily Mills Co.	Scan Yarn Co.
P.O. Box 326	Dept. HWH	P.O. Box 384
Stonington, **Connecticut** 06378	Shelby, **North Carolina**	Westerly, **Rhode Island** 02891

Shuttlecraft
P.O. Box 6041
Providence 4, **Rhode Island**

Troy Yarn and Textile Co.
603 Mineral Spring Ave.
Pawtucket, **Rhode Island** 02860

The Maysville Co. For Cotton warp
ordered through—
Sears Roebuck & Co.

looms & equipment

Gilmore Looms
1032 North Broadway Ave.
Stockton, **California** 95205

Structo Division
King-Seeley Thermos Co.
Freeport, **Illinois**

L. W. Macomber
166 Essex Street
Saugus, **Massachusetts**

The Norwood Loom Co.
Box 272
Baldwin, **Michigan** 49304

Nilus Leclerc
L'Isletville 6, Quebec, **Canada**

Kessenick Looms
7463 Harwood Ave.
Wauwatosa 13, **Wisconsin**

dyes

Putnam Fadeless Dyes
Monroe Chemical Co.
301 Oak Street
Quincy, **Illinois** 62302

Cushing's Perfection Dyes
W. Cushing & Co.
Dover-Foxcroft, **Maine** 04426

Tintex and Rit dyes obtainable at five
and dime stores.

general suppliers

School Products Co.
312 East 23rd Street
New York, **New York** 10010

The Silver Shuttle
1301 35th Street N.W.
Washington, D.C. 20007

SCHOOL DIRECTORY

The following list of professional schools, universities, and workshops offer summer courses for the beginning and more advanced weaver. All the schools listed operate on a year-round basis except those marked with an asterisk*. Those so marked have no summer courses at present. For further information, write to the school direct.

Mendocino Art Center
Box 36
Mendocino, **California**

Grae-Ries Workshops
424 La Verne,
Mill Valley, **California**

Pasadena City College
1570 East Colorado Boulevard
Pasadena, **California**

The Yarn Depot, Inc.
545 Sutter Street
San Francisco, **California**

Brookfield Craft Center, Inc.
Brookfield, **Connecticut**

Willimantic State College
Willimantic, **Connecticut**

School of the Art Institute
of Chicago
Michigan at Adams
Chicago, **Illinois**

Indiana University
Fine Arts Department
Bloomington, **Indiana**

Wichita Art Association
9112 East Central
Wichita, **Kansas**

*Berea College
Art Department
Berea, **Kentucky**

Haystack Mountain School
of Crafts
Deer Isle, **Maine**

*Cranbrook Academy of Art
500 Lone Pine Road
Bloomfield Hills, **Michigan**

Art School of the Crafts Guild
380–168th Avenue, S.W., R4
Holland, **Michigan**

Northern Michigan University
Marquette, **Michigan**

University of New Hampshire
Department of the Arts
Durham, **New Hampshire**

Newark Museum Arts Workshop
43–49 Washington Street
Newark, **New Jersey**

Chautauqua Art Center
Chautauqua, **New York**

Thousand Islands Museum
Clayton, **New York**

Craft Students League
West Side Branch YWCA
840 Eighth Avenue
New York, **New York**

Fashion Institute of Technology
227 West 27th Street
New York, **New York**

School for American Craftsmen
Rochester Institute of Technology
65 Plymouth Avenue South
Rochester, **New York**

Woodstock Guild of Craftsmen
P.O. Box 95
Woodstock, **New York**

John C. Campbell Folk School
Brasstown, **North Carolina**

Penland School of Crafts
Penland, **North Carolina**

Cleveland Institute of Art
11141 East Boulevard
Cleveland, **Ohio**

Moore College of Art
20th and Race Streets
Philadelphia, **Pennsylvania**

Philadelphia College of Textiles
and Science
School House Lane and Henry Avenue
Philadelphia, **Pennsylvania**

Pennsylvania State University
Department of Arts
210 Arts Building
University Park, **Pennsylvania**

University of Tennessee
Pi Beta Phi Settlement School
Gatlinburg, **Tennessee**

*East Tennessee State University
Department of Art
Johnson City, **Tennessee**

Fletcher Farm Craft School
Ludlow, **Vermont**

Fidalgo Allied Arts
La Conner, **Washington**

*West Virginia University
Morgantown, **West Virginia**